# KIDS' TV

## The First 25 Years

# KIDS' TV

## The First 25 Years

## Stuart Fischer

**Facts On File Publications**
460 Park Avenue South
New York, N.Y. 10016

# KIDS' TV
# THE FIRST 25 YEARS

**Library of Congress Cataloging in
Publication Data**

Fischer, Stuart.
  Kids' TV.

  Includes index.
  1. Television programs for children — United
States — History and criticism.''      I. Title.
PN1992.8.C46F5      791.45'75      82-7382
ISBN 0-87196-794-4      AACR2

Printed in the United States of America

10 9 8 7 6 5 4 3 2 1

To Sy Fischer

# Contents

## Acknowledgments

I would like to express my appreciation to the following persons and corporations for volunteering their time and services during the preparation of this book: Joe Barbera; William Hanna; Stan Lee; David DePatie; Fritz Freleng; Bob Clampett; Paul Winchell; Shari Lewis; John Goldwater; Henry G. Sapperstein; Lou Scheimer; Chuck Jones; Jack Barry; Mark Wilson; Burr Tillstrom; Don Herbert; Ed Graham; Hal Seeger; Pinky Lee; Sy Fischer; Claude Kirchner; Buster Crabbe; Paul Tripp; Bil Baird; Morey Bunin; Theodore Schulte; Arthur Rankin; Jules Bass; Jack Spear; Jay Ward; Bill Scott; Ed McMahon; Treadwell Covington; Art Scott; Ray Chan; Don Hastings; Bob Hastings; Al Brodax; Sonny Fox; Mary Hartline; Hanna-Barbera Productions; Filmation Associates; Marvel Comics Group; MCA Inc.; Paramount Pictures Corporation; MGM; Warner Communications, Inc.; King Features Syndicate; Robert Keeshan Associates; ITC Entertainment; Krofft Entertainment; Rankin-Bass Productions; Viacom International; The Wrather Corporation; Harvey Publications; Twentieth Century-Fox Film Corporation; and Archie Comics Publications.

# Introduction

Children's television really began with the *Howdy Doody* show, which debuted in 1947 and ran for 13 years. That show marked the beginning an era of television whose impact can still be felt in the children's television programming of today. Since Howdy Doody made his first appearance, three generations of children have found heroes and role models, fantasies and laughter, in images on the video screen. Just as adults over 40 remember every detail of the radio serials of their youth, younger adults still remember the name of Sky King's airplane (Songbird), what Andy used to tell Froggy on *Andy's Gang* ("Twang your magic twanger, Froggy"), and the name of Rocky and Bullwinkle's home town (Frostbite Falls).

The longevity of some children's programs is unparalleled in television history. *Captain Kangaroo*, for example, first aired in 1955 and has been part of the lives of American kids ever since. The continuing success of this show can be attributed to its gentle blend of fantasy and reality. This imaginative synthesis explains the success of many children's shows, even though styles of programming have changed enormously over the years.

The first decade of children's programming began with group participation as a dominant theme. Shows like *Juvenile Jury, Captain Video and His Video Rangers* and *Birthday Party* were broadcast live with an adult host, and often involved audience participation. People watching those early shows carefully might have caught a glimpse of some of today's well-known personalities making their TV debuts. Ed McMahon of *The Tonight Show*, for example, was a clown in *The Big Top* (1950—1957); Don Knotts was Tim Tremble of *Howdy Doody*, and Cliff Robertson was the hero of *Rod Brown, Rocket Ranger* (1953—1954).

As the medium grew, participation shows began to give way to real-life adventure stories. The popularity of shows like *Fury* (1955—1966), *My Friend Flicka* (1956—1958), *Adventures of Robin Hood* (1955—1958), and *Tales of the Texas Rangers*

(1955—1959) led to more sophisticated children's programming, sparked by the recognition that children were an important target for advertisers.

After this realization, it wasn't long before the appearance of animated characters that doubled as advertising symbols of particular products. Television had always been used to sell merchandise to children—Mickey Mouse ears and patches were popular items in the 1950s—but in the mid-1960s characters created for advertising figured prominently in children's programs. They frequently sold the sponsor's products within the context of the show itself. For example, Linus the Lion-hearted, first created by the advertising agency of Benton & Bowles as a character to represent General Foods products in their commercials, became the focus of an animated children's series. He was joined by two other characters representing General Foods breakfast cereals—Sugar Bear and the Postman. The series became so important and lucrative to General Foods that the company insisted on production standards far beyond what was customary at that time. The costs of the half-hour show often ran three times that of any other equivalent cartoon series, and the voices of the characters were provided by such famous performers as Sheldon Leonard, Carl Reiner, and Jonathan Winters.

However, in 1969 Linus the Lion-hearted was canceled, in part because government agencies ruled that children watching the show could not distinguish sufficiently between the commercials and the show's content. This problem reappeared in 1969 with the Saturday morning show Hot Wheels, sponsored by Mattel Toys, which also sold an entire line of toy cars by the same name. Again, the Federal Trade Commission and the Federal Communications Commission frowned on this kind of 30-minute commercial. Although neither agency brought legal action, they did pressure Mattel into withdrawing its sponsorship, resulting in the show's cancellation in 1971.

The lesson was not lost on other advertisers.

The advent of color television in the early 1960s opened the medium of television to the fantasy world of animation. A cavalcade of animated characters paraded across the screen on Saturday mornings and on the early hours of weekday prime time. The networks and sponsors were quick to recognize the unlimited potential this brought to children's programming; some of these shows even crossed over to captivate the adult audience and have since become perennial syndicated favorites. Shows like The Flintstones, The Pink Panther, Bugs Bunny, and Yogi Bear are still aired during the hours devoted to children's programming; they also appear occasionally in prime-time animated specials.

During the 1960s and 1970s, many cartoon programs developed very large audiences. Advertisers and merchandisers sought to capitalize on this popularity, competing for advertising time on the shows and the rights to license the cartoon characters for use on such products as lunchboxes, notebooks and shirts. And as the children raised on cartoons grew older, they became an eager audience for animated, feature-length films such as Fritz the Cat (made by Ralph Bakshi, who got his start directing Deputy Dawg for Terrytoons).

Animated cartoons have come to reflect American popular culture. The pop music explosion found its way to Saturday mornings on a number of animated shows, including The Archies, Josie and the Pussycats, The Banana Splits, The Beatles and The Monkees. Human singers frequently released hit singles under the names of the characters in these shows. Music had become a large part of growing up in America, and these cartoons were television's response to this development.

The 1960s also witnessed a growing awareness of racial differences. The children's programming of this period made sincere efforts to avoid racial stereotypes and foster positive values. As children's TV producers and directors became more concerned with the needs of their audience, they broadened the scope of their characters and themes.

Consider a show like *Fat Albert and the Cosby Kids*, in which the animated stars were all minority children who were forever helping kids (and occasionally adults) to identify problems and solve them before they got out of hand. This show was (and still is) an enormous financial success; more importantly, it demonstrates the viability of children's programming as a learning tool.

Many other trends in society are reflected in children's programming of the 1960s. The country's fascination with technology, space travel, and galactic adventure gave rise to a number of science-fiction adventure shows, notably *Space Ghost* and *The Fantastic Four*. The line between science-fiction and superhero shows, another development of the period, was often indistinct, resulting in shows like *Space Kidettes*, which involved a group of young, crime-fighting crusaders operating in outer space. The superhero shows were popular but practically begged to be parodied—and they soon were, most

notably in the cartoon series *Underdog*. Espionage, a popular theme in adult television, was also adapted for child audiences. A good example is the comic character Secret Squirrel, who was derived from Ian Fleming's James Bond and appeared on the screen wearing an oversized trench coat with the collar turned up; he operated under the code name Agent 000. Secret Squirrel's nemesis was an evil character called Yellowpinky, an obvious allusion to the Goldfinger, the famous Bond villain. A more direct parody of adult television appeared on Saturday morning in the cartoon *Tom of T.H.U.M.B.* (Tiny Humans Underground Military Bureau), which was inspired by the adult hit series *The Man from U.N.C.L.E.*

This book—with entries on every children's show to air on network television during the medium's first 25 years—traces the history of children's programming and, I hope, brings to life some of the great old shows and characters so many of us grew up watching.

SF
Hollywood, California

# KIDS' TV

## The First 25 Years

1946-1947 Season

## BIRTHDAY PARTY

**Thursday,** *7:30 — 8:00 p.m.: Dumont*
**Debut:** *5/15/47; **Cancellation:** 6/23/49*
**Producer:** *George Scheck*
**Hosts:** *Ted Brown, Bill Slater (1947), Aunt Grace (1948)*

This show offered weekly birthday parties for visiting youngsters from the audience. All the necessary ingredients were here: ice cream and cookies, games and performances by talented youngsters. And, of course, a cake.

The simple stories told on the show were tailored to preschool children. Ted Brown frequently dressed as King Cole, and the show was known informally as "King Cole's Birthday Party" for that reason. Children sent in photos and information about themselves in the hope that George Scheck would pick them from the hundreds of applicants.

Surprise guests included the Mayor of New York, Vincent Inpellitteri. The show evolved into the much different *Star Time.* The spin-off originally aired on NBC and later went to Dumont.

George Scheck, who also produced *Star Time,* was responsible for two variety series, *Doorway to Fame* and *Boardwalk.* Scheck is now an artists' manager and has been involved in the careers of such people as Connie Francis, Bernadette Peters (then known as LaZare), Barry Gordon and Leslie Uggams. All had at one time appeared on *Birthday Party.*

*Birthday Party:* young enthusiastic participants thronging the Mayor of New York..(Courtesy of George Scheck.)

## JUVENILE JURY

*Thursday, 8:00–8:30 p.m.: NBC, CBS*
*Debut: 4/3/47; Cancellation: 10/3/53*
  *(NBC)*
*Return: 10/11/53; Cancellation: 9/14/54*
  *(CBS)*
*Return: 1/2/55; Cancellation: 3/27/55*
  *(NBC)*
*Producers: Jack Barry, Dan Enright*
*Host/Announcer: Jack Barry*

This children's game show featured a panel of five youngsters who were asked to give opinions on how to solve a given problem. These problems would be suggested to the panel either by the studio audience or by viewers.

Jack Barry and co-producer Dan Enright developed the concept at New York radio station WOR. Barry had been active in radio, having worked for a number of stations in Chicago and Trenton, New Jersey. *Juvenile Jury* originated as a radio series in 1946 and was broadcast by the Mutual Broadcasting System. It transferred to network television in 1947 as a 16-week summer series, and subsequently went on to become a prime-time success. This game show has the distinction of being the first commercially sponsored network series, with General Foods as the sponsor. It left prime-time in 1954 but continued on Sunday afternoons until 1955.

*Juvenile Jury* served as the launching pad for Barry's and Enright's television careers. They went on to create **Winky Dink and You** (1953–54) again hosted by Jack Barry. Their company, Barry & Enright Productions, has produced many successful game shows, including *Tic Tac Dough, The Joker's Wild* and *Twenty One.* Barry and Enright recently entered motion pictures with the successful *Private Lessons.*

## SMALL FRY CLUB

*Tuesday, 7:00–8:00 p.m.: Dumont*
*Debut: 3/11/47; Cancellation: 6/15/51*
*Producer: Bob and Kay Emery*
*Host: Bob Emery*

In 1947 Big Brother Bob Emery moved into television from a successful radio programming career. The Dumont network, headed by Alan B. Dumont, competed fiercely with other networks for a young audience, one that would maintain an allegiance to this fourth network as it grew to maturity. *Movies For Small Fry* presented film classics, narrated by Emery. With the move to a daily schedule the show's format was altered to that of a "club," participated in by a young studio audience. The program offered a diversity of entertainment, including cartoons, sketches, songs and, after 1949, puppet shows. Every character or situation contributed to the upright moral stance adopted by Bob and his wife Kay. Segments dealt with manners, self-discipline, health and nutrition.

The show enjoyed widespread popularity. It was difficult to obtain spectator tickets. At the close of its network run, Emery returned to station WBZ in Boston, where he hosted *The Big Brother Bob Emery Show.*

Prior to joining Dumont, Emery had created and hosted a radio show, *Triple B Ranch,* which introduced Buffalo Bob Smith to television. Smith went on to host the highly successful **Howdy Doody** (1947/48). Emery also hosted a local New York television show called *The Rainbow Club.* This "amateur hour" introduced, among others, Vic Damone and Beverly Sills.

*Small Fry Club*: "Big Brother" Bob Emery; Honey, the Bunny; Willie the Wiz; Mr. Mischief, the Panda; and Peppy, the Penguin. (Courtesy of Wally Dodash.)

1947-1948 Season

# HOWDY DOODY

**Saturday,** *5:00 – 6:00 p.m.: NBC*
**Debut:** *12/27/47; Cancellation: 9/24/60*
**Executive Producers:** *Roger Muir, Martin Stone*
**Narrator:** *Dayton Allen (for the film segment)*
**Puppeteers:** *Rhoda Mann, Lee Carney*
**Voices:** *Bob Smith (Howdy Doody), Dayton Allen (Phineas T. Bluster), Allen Swift, Herb Vigran*

*Cast*
Buffalo Bob Smith . . . . . . . .Bob Smith
Clarabell Hornblow . . . . . . .Bob Keeshan
                                Bob Nicholson
                                Lou Anderson
The Story Princess . . . . . . . .Alene Dalton
Tim Tremble . . . . . . . . . . . .Don Knotts
Chief Thunderthud . . . . . . .Bill Lecornec
Princess Summer-Fall-
    Winter-Spring . . . . . . . . .Judy Tyler
Lowell Thomas, Jr. . . . . . . .Himself
**Additional characters:** *Doctor Sing-A-Song, Grandpa Doody Puppet, Dr. Jose Bluster, Double Doody, Heidi Doody, Ugly Sam, Lanky Lou, Trigger Happy, Spin Platter, The Flubadub, Inspector John, Captain Scuttlebut, The Bloop, Dilly Dally, Sandy McTavish, Andy Handy, Doc Ditto, Sandra, the witch.*

*Question:* "Say kids, What time is it?"
*Answer:* "It's How-w-w-wdy Doody Time!" came the cheerful response each week, heralding another episode of what many consider to be the most popular children's series in the history of broadcasting.

Set in the colorful town of "Doodyville," the series revolved around the antics of a circus troupe led by Buffalo Bob Smith, who dressed in a pioneer outfit and resembled the legendary Buffalo Bill. His marionette, Howdy Doody, a freckle-faced, puffy-cheeked little boy with a wide grin, was always at Buffalo Bob's side. Their comic nemesis was Phineas T. Bluster, a grumpy

old man who objected to people having fun. *Doodyville* was populated by a colorful assortment of puppets and people who made brief appearances, as in a circus. Each episode was comprised of a silent film short, one or two songs, and a story involving the characters of Doodyville. An audience of children watched each episode from the bleachers, otherwise referred to as "The Peanut Gallery."

The series first aired as *Puppet Playhouse Presents,* a title amended to *Howdy Doody* after only one week. It initially ran on NBC for one hour every Saturday, but the show's popularity grew swiftly, and the network began programming it twice and later three times a week. Finally, *Howdy Doody* became a daily show, airing Mondays through Fridays for 30 minutes. This schedule began in March/April 1948, less than a year after the program's debut, making it the first daytime "strip" show in TV history. It continued to run five days a week until 1956, when the network shifted it to Saturday mornings, where it remained until its demise in 1960. The move was dictated not because of a decline in popularity, but because the program was taking up too much time on NBC's schedule. The network needed greater variety in the line-up, as did their advertisers.

Among those responsible for the creation of *Howdy Doody* were Roger Muir and his superior at NBC, Warner Wade. They had met in the army, where Muir, a photographer by training, worked on military films. In 1946, he joined NBC in part at the invitation of Wade. Muir assisted in the establishment of the NBC News department and produced and directed many early shows, including the World Series telecasts. Muir discovered Bob Smith on an NBC Saturday morning radio show titled *Triple B Ranch.* Smith, singer and co-host of the program, had created a character called Elmer, whose opening words for each show were- "How-w-w-wdy Doody." Here was Muir's acorn. Recruiting Smith and establishing the character Howdy Doody, they went into production in the RCA Building in New York.

The original "Howdy Doody" puppet was designed by Frank Paris. After Paris left the show, the dummy was redesigned by three artists formerly employed by Walt Disney Studios: Norman Blackburn, Mel Shaw and Velma Dawson. Among the actors on the legendary show (most of whom have faded from memory), is Bob Keeshan, better known as Captain Kangaroo. Keeshan was one of three actors who at various times played Clarabell the clown. The other two were Bob Nicholson and Lou Anderson. Keeshan left *Howdy Doody* in 1953 to launch his own now-famous show on CBS. Martin Stone, listed as an executive producer of the show, was in reality Bob Smith's agent. Sensing the potential for Howdy Doody tie-in merchandise, he established the Kagren company to exploit these lucrative rights. The result was a deluge of licenses for dolls, records, toys and all manner of items that carried the name and likeness of the freckle-faced, blue-eyed six-year-old boy.

Of the many characters who made their debut on the *Howdy Doody* show, none is so memorable as *Gumby*. This little green clay figure, the brainchild of Art Clokey, went on to his own series in 1956 and starred in a stop-motion animated film.

In its 13-year run, *Howdy Doody* played 2,343 television performances. It was also featured on radio, where it ran on Saturday mornings from 1952 to 1958. In all, the show played more than 3,000 times. It was sponsored by such prominent advertisers as Marx Toys, Kellogg's, Mars, Ideal Toys, General Foods, and many others. In 1976 a new syndicated version of the show, hosted as before by Bob Smith, failed to capture the magic of its predecessor and was short-lived. Smith now lives in Florida.

# LUCKY PUP

*Monday—Friday, 6:30–6:45 p.m.: CBS*
*Debut: 8/23/48; Cancellation: 6/23/51*
*Producers: Hope and Morey Bunin, Lloyd Gross, Clarence Schimmel*
*Puppeteers: Hope and Morey Bunin*
*Hostess: Doris Brown*

This much-loved puppet show revolved around the misadventures of the "Kindness Club." The series was hosted by Doris Brown, the only human member of the show.

Lucky Pup was a cute dog/puppet, who inherited $5 million from the estate of a circus queen. The setting was a circus. Lucky Pup was accompanied by such characters as Jolo, the resident clown, and Foodini, the villain and wicked magician who devised innumerable schemes to separate Lucky from his inheritance. Foodini was assisted by Pinhead, a dim but loyal accomplice.

As the series progressed the empathy of viewers shifted from Pup to Foodini and Pinhead, and they eventually became the focus of the series. Pup was too "goody-two-shoes." *Lucky Pup* was originally programmed for two weeks in the 8:00–9:00 p.m. evening schedule, to enable an adult audience to review the show's honorable intentions. The series was then shifted to the daily schedule. *Lucky Pup* went off the air when hostess Doris Brown was married. Morey and Hope Bunin returned to the small screen the following season with a spin-off, titled **Foodini, the Great** (1949–50), starring the two "ne'er do wells" of the earlier show.

The Bunins first appeared on television in 1944, on an experimental station in Boston. From there they moved to New York with their puppets. They guest-starred on numerous shows, in addition to making appearances at Radio City Music Hall. Morey and Hope have toured overseas and have entertained at various USO shows, clubs, and summer camps. Their theater appearances have brought them an enthusiastic and loyal audience.

Pinhead and Foodini. (Courtesy Morey Bunin.)

## SCRAPBOOK JR. EDITION

*Sunday, 6:00–6:30 p.m.:* CBS
*Debut: 6/27/48; Cancellation: 11/14/48*
*Hosts:* Jini Boyd O'Connor, Scotty Mac-
   Gregor
*Producer:* Gil Fates

This was a fairly sophisticated general-knowledge quiz show. Audiences participated by supplying examples of their hobbies. That hobby was the subject of the competition. There was also a puzzle-tune segment, in which contestants were obliged to maintain complete concentration to identify songs.

More often than not the prizes were lavish, ranging from bicycles to pets. *Scrapbook Jr. Edition* began life as a local New York show in October 1947 and subsequently moved to the CBS network. The show moved from Sunday evenings to Sunday afternoons, where it remained until May 1949.

## WINCHELL AND MAHONEY

*Saturday, 30 Minutes:* Dumont
*Debut: 6/47; Cancellation: 9/47*
*Host:* Paul Winchell

The year 1947 marked the birth of children's programming on television and the initial appearance of ventriloquist Paul Winchell and his puppet Jerry Mahoney, one of the most popular acts in the history of television. This series, which ran for 13 weeks over the Dumont network (no longer in existence), was filmed and transmitted from makeshift studios in the Wanamaker department store in lower Manhattan. These were television's pioneer days and not many people yet owned a home "video set," as they were then called. Servel refrigerators sponsored the program and insisted that their product be prominently displayed. Consequently, Winchell performed comedy routines centering on a Servel refrigerator, using a variety of appealing foods as props.

Winchell had become a ventriloquist at the age of 14, after answering an advertisement for "the secrets of ventriloquism—for only a dime." In 1935, while a student at New York's School of Industrial Arts, he built himself a partner in the form of Jerry Mahoney. Jerry measured 42 inches in height and weighed close to 20 pounds. They were inseparable artistically, of course, and together they enjoyed a long career that began in radio. They had made their debut in that medium in 1936 on *Major Bowes Original Amateur Hour,* hosted by Edward E. Bowes. Following his TV debut, Winchell appeared on various variety programs, performing his routine with Jerry on *The Milton Berle Show* and Ed Sullivan's *Toast of the Town,* among many others. Although his first series had only a limited run, it was followed by many longer running series including: **Dunninger and Winchell** (1948), **The Paul Winchell and Jerry Mahoney Spiedel Show** (1950), **Jerry Mahoney's Club House** (1954), **Toyland Express** (1955), **Circus Time** (1956), **The Paul Winchell Show** (1957), **Cartoonsville** (1963) and **Runaround** (1972).

During Winchell's early performances with Mahoney, the puppet would frequently refer to an unseen friend of his, Knucklehead Smith. In 1951, Winchell finally brought Knucklehead into being, introducing him on *The Paul Winchell and Jerry Mahoney Spiedel Show.* Younger than Jerry, Knucklehead was about the same height and weight. After many references to "my friend," the public's curiosity had to be satisfied.

The host of many popular shows dating back to television's infancy, Winchell has also made many commercials and provided the voices for hundreds of television cartoon characters. During the 1981–82 season, Winchell was heard as the voice of *Gargamel* in Hanna-Barbera's Saturday morning cartoon, *The Smurfs.*

In January, 1980, Winchell presented Jerry Mahoney to the permanent collection of the Smithsonian Institution, and in July, 1982, Knucklehead Smith joined him there. The puppets represent a pioneering era in television programming for children.

In addition to being a performer, Winchell is a prolific inventor who has contributed significantly to medical science. He became interested in medicine while performing at various camp and hospital shows. In the 1950s, Winchell worked at local hospitals while studying at Columbia University. He eventually earned a D.S. degree in the field of biomedical engineering. In 1963, he designed and patented a mechanical heart while participating in the artificial heart program at the University of Utah's Medical School. As of 1982 the Food and Drug Administration has given permission for his artificial heart to be used in humans. Winchell has also designed a surgical suit to reduce body temperature of patients during surgery, and a blood plasma defroster.

*Winchell and Mahoney*: Paul Winchell with Jerry Mahoney (left) and Knucklehead Smith. (Courtesy of Paul Winchell.)

1948-1949 Season

# ADVENTURES OF OKY DOKY

*Thursday,* 7:00 – 7:30 p.m.: *Dumont*
*Debut:* 11/4/48; *Cancellation:* 5/26/49
*Producer:* Frank Bunetta
*Hostess:* Wendy Barrie
*Puppeteer and voice of Oky Doky:* Dayton
    Allen

This Dumont series was one of television's first children's shows. It was derived from *Tots, Tweens and Teens,* a local New York, youth-oriented fashion program. It went network as *Adventures of Oky Doky,* later retitled *Oky Doky Ranch.*

Oky Doky was a 30-inch mustached marionette, created by Raye Copeland. The show was staged on a dude ranch, where youngsters visited Oky and participated in games and junior talent contests. In addition, they would be treated to the puppet's Wild-West adventures. The show was far from tranquil, with knock-down, drag-out battles occurring frequently. Fists and furniture flew whenever Oky confronted less scrupulous visitors. The puppet invariably emerged victorious, thanks to his magic strength pills. This was a wholesome milk-based product, a reminder of the importance of a healthy diet.

Launched as a half-hour Thursday-night show, the series was subsequently reformatted as a twice weekly 15-minute program, aired on Tuesdays *and* Thursdays. *Oky Doky* was produced at the Wanamaker Department Store in lower Manhattan. Space was frequently leased to television producers during the early years of broadcasting.

Dayton Allen eventually left the show to join **Howdy Doody** (1947/48), where he was responsible for the puppets and voices. From *Howdy Doody* he went on to supporting roles in *Winky Dink and You, Versatile Varieties* and *Lancelot Link/Secret Chimp,* for which he provided several voices. Allen has also been heard in radio and television commercials. In addition to this children's show, producer Frank Bunetta has worked often with Jackie Gleason. The concept for the series came, in part, from Marcy Fink.

# CAPTAIN VIDEO AND HIS VIDEO RANGERS

*Monday-Friday,* 7:00 – 7:30 p.m.: *Dumont*
*Debut:* 6/27/49; *Cancellation:* 4/1/55
*Creator/Writer:* M. C. Brock
*Production Executive:* James Caddigan

## Cast

Captain Video . . . . . . . . . .Richard Coogan
                        (*1949 – 50*),
                        Al Hodge
                        (*1951 – 55*)
The Video Ranger . . . . . . .Don Hastings
Dr. Pauli . . . . . . . . . . . . . . .Hal Conklin

This legendary low-budget series was television's first science fiction program.

It was set in the year 2254 A.D. Captain Video, the self-proclaimed "Guardian of the Universe," operated out of a mountaintop laboratory, with the assistance of his young Video Ranger. The Captain was equipped with the latest technology and devastating firepower (which stunned rather than killed). His hardware was more often than not made of dime-store cardboard and paste props, whose effectiveness owed much to the imaginations of young viewers. The space hero's adversaries included Nargola, Mook the Moon Man, Kul of Eos, Heng Foo Seng, and, the most deadly of all, Dr. Pauli. Video's nemesis was the leader of the Astroidal Society. Like the Captain (but for less commendable reasons), he was always seeking new, sophisticated weaponry.

A number of now-famous actors appeared in this series. Ernest Borgnine played the evil Nargola, and Tony Randall and Jack Klugman were cast as ne'er-do-wells. They were united again in the 1970s as the co-stars of the TV series, *The Odd Couple.*

Captain Video was portrayed by two actors during the series' six-year run. In 1950 Richard Coogan relinquished the role to Al Hodge, who had been the voice of radio's

*The Green Hornet.* Hodge turned the series into a major success, but at the expense of his own career. When the show left the air, he had become so identified with the role of the Captain that he was unable to find other parts. He died penniless in a New York City hotel in March 1979. Don Hastings, the young Video Ranger, made his mark in daytime soap operas. His first was *Edge of Night,* followed by *As the World Turns,* in which he has appeared for the past 21 years.

Larry White and David Lowe, two of the show's directors, went on to major roles in television. White served as president of Columbia Pictures Television and subsequently became an independent producer. His most recent credit is the miniseries *The Blue and The Gray.* Lowe is an award-winning producer on *CBS Reports.* Sponsors for the show included Powerhouse Candy Bars and Post cereals.

Broadcast live with filmed sequences, the show originated from a studio in Manhattan's Wanamaker Department Store. Production was subsequently moved uptown to the new Dumont studios on East 67th Street. Old Western films were shown via the Captain's "Remote Tele-Carrier." The cowboys were billed as the Captain's cohorts in his battle against interplanetary injustice, but they were only there as an inexpensive way to fill up air time.

In 1953 the series was cut back to once a week and retitled *The Secret Files of Captain Video.* After the program was cancelled in 1956, Hodge returned that year as the host of *Captain Video's Cartoons,* a weekly animated cartoon series shown in syndication. A third Captain, Judd Holdren, appeared in a 15-episode movie serial released in 1951.

Ted Bergman, head of the Dumont network prior to its demise, was instrumental in the success of Captain Video. Bergman went on to produce *Three's Company,* one of television's most popular series and a sitcom trend-setter.

## CARTOON TELETALES

*Sunday, 6:00 – 6:30 p.m.: ABC*
*Debut: 11/14/48; Cancellation: 9/24/50*
*Producer: Chuck and Jack Luchsinger*

The brothers Chuck and Jack Luchsinger used a sketchpad to illustrate their children's stories, which they called "Cartoon Teletales." Jack served as narrator while Chuck did quick pencil renderings of a host of colorful characters. Among their diverse creations were Usta, the rooster; Bumsniff, the bloodhound; Madcap, the mountain goat; Mimi, the mole, and many others.

This series first aired locally in Philadelphia in 1948. It moved to New York as a late afternoon show in June of that year. In November it moved into an early evening network slot, where it remained for the duration of its run.

## THE CHILDREN'S HOUR

*Sunday, 10:30 – 11:30 a.m.: NBC*
*Debut: 1/30/49; Cancellation: 5/26/57*
*Producer: Alice Clements*
*Host/Announcer: Ed Herlihy*

This variety series, a showcase for young talent, was originally conceived for radio in 1929. Its guiding light was Alice Clements, who operated an advertising agency with her husband. One of the team's major accounts was *Horn and Hardart,* for whom Mrs. Clements produced and scripted the show.

The original hosts of the radio show were Paul Douglas and Ralph Edwards, the latter now a prominent game-show producer. In 1940 their places were taken by Ed Herlihy, who survived the move to television. Many now-famous performers made their initial appearances on this program, as children. The list includes Bernadette Peters, Beverly Sills, Joey Heatherton, Ken Howard, Stuart Ostrow, Gregory Hines and Jaqueline Cortney.

*The Children's Hour:* Ed Herlihy and friend. (Courtesy of Alice Clements.)

Host Ed Herlihy was often up-staged by his "human" dog Marrowbone, played by "Cricket" Skilling. After 29 years in both media, the show left the air in 1957. Herlihy continues to be active in television, under-taking voice-overs and appearing on talk shows. After 35 years, he continues to be Kraft's product spokesman.

# CHILD'S WORLD

*Tuesday, 7:30–7:45 p.m.: ABC*
*Debut: 11/1/48; Cancellation: 4/27/49*
*Producer: Helen Parkhurst*
*Host: Helen Parkhurst*

Modeled after Helen Parkhurst's radio program, *Child's World* encouraged children to discuss important topics. It was set in Ms. Parkhurst's apartment, where a small group of eight- to 13-year-olds discussed such topics as jealousy, prejudice and religion. This unrehearsed and live production was provocative and innovative. Unfortunately, it lasted for less than six months.

# DUNNINGER AND WINCHELL
(Also known as **The Bigelow Show**)

*Thursday, 9:30–10:00 p.m.: NBC*
*Wednesday, 9:00–9:30 p.m.: CBS*
*Debut: 10/14/48; Cancellation: 9/28/49*
  *(NBC)*
*Return: 10/5/49; Cancellation: 12/28/49*
  *(CBS)*
*Producer: Martin Stone*
*Hosts: Paul Winchell, Joseph Dunninger*

This series was actually two shows in one. Fifteen minutes belonged to ventriloquist Paul Winchell and his wise-cracking puppet companion, Jerry Mahoney. The other half was devoted to mentalist Joseph Dunninger.

Winchell and Mahoney performed their usual knock-about routine with an occasional visit from a guest star. Winchell came to this show after his TV debut in **Winchell and Mahoney** (1947/48). He frequently appeared as a guest on such shows as Ed Sullivan's *Toast of the Town* and *The Milton Berle Show*.

Joseph Dunninger was the most famous mind-reader of his day, and his remarkable ability baffled and confused audiences. On one historic telecast, Dunninger, in a New York studio, voiced the thoughts of a United States Congressman standing on the steps of the Capitol in Washington. This was aired live, with both men appearing simulta-neously on a split screen.

The show was sponsored by Bigelow Rugs, hence its alternate title.

# JUDY SPLINTERS

*Monday-Friday, 7:00–7:15 p.m.: NBC*
*Debut: 6/13/49; Cancellation: 6/30/50*
*Producer: Roger Muir*
*Host: Shirley Dinsdale*
*Puppeteer: Shirley Dinsdale*

Shirley Dinsdale, a 21-year-old ventriloquist, and her pig-tailed puppet, "Judy Splinters,"

were the hosts of this live program, which was a summer replacement for **Kukla, Fran and Ollie** (1948/49).

*Judy Splinters* was first seen in 1949 as a local show on station KNBH in Los Angeles. It subsequently moved to Chicago for a network summer run. The show brought Ms. Dinsdale an Emmy Award (she was television's first recipient), and it moved to New York for nine months as an afternoon show in the 1949–50 season. Although the show left network prime-time on August 5th, 1949, it continued in the afternoon until the following year.

In addition to being both host and puppeteer, Ms. Dinsdale contributed to the writing. Roger Muir was also executive producer of **Howdy Doody** (1947/48).

## KUKLA, FRAN AND OLLIE

*Monday-Friday, 7:00 – 7:30 p.m.: NBC*
*Debut: 11/29/48; Cancellation: 8/31/57*
*Producer: Burr Tillstrom*
*Puppeteer: Burr Tillstrom*
*Announcer: Hugh Downs*

*Kukla, Fran and Ollie*: Fran Allison with the Kuklapolitan Players, as they appeared in the 1970s. (Courtesy of Burr Tillstrom.)

*Regulars:* Carolyn Gilbert, Caesar Giovan-
nini

Burr Tillstrom was the creator, voice and
puppeteer of this landmark series. It has run
in various lengths and formats, on network
television, in syndication and on Public
Television. The program's many awards include a Peabody in 1949 and an Emmy in
1953.

Kukla, a worried-looking glove-puppet
with a clown's nose, is the founding member
of the Kuklapolitan Players. Tillstrom had
created Kukla in 1936 as a "natural extension" of his own personality. (Kukla is the
Russian diminutive for doll.) Kukla's foil is
Oliver J. Dragon, or just plain Ollie, an out-
going dragon with a big velvet mouth and
one big tooth. Tillstrom and his puppets
made their first network appearance under
the auspices of RCA at the New York
World's Fair of 1939–40. They participated
in NBC's initial TV broadcasts and appeared
regularly at the RCA exhibit.

Fran Allison, a Chicago-based radio
celebrity, had first met Tillstrom's minitroupe
at a political rally just before World War II. In
1947 Tillstrom got his own television series
on local station WBKB. He needed a spontaneous human "straight man" to respond
to, and Fran Allison fit the bill.

Members of Tillstrom's company at various times have included: Fletcher Rabbit, a
bunny with droopy ears; Madame Ophelia
Oglepuss, a haughty former opera star;
Beulah Witch, a one-time student of elec-
tronics who now rides a jet-propelled
broomstick; Cecil Bill, a stage manager with
a language all his own; Colonel Crackie, a
long-winded Southern gentleman; Delores
Dragon, Ollie's infant relative; and Olivia,
his elderly mother, whose hair was a stagger-
ing 75 feet long.

The program followed the day-to-day activities of the Kuklapolitans. Often the
Players would stage their own lavish productions, ranging from satires like *Martin
Dragon, Private Tooth* to such operettas as
*The Mikado.* Original musical productions
also were presented, including *St. George*
and the Dragon. For the latter, broadcast in
June, 1953, the Players were accompanied
by Arthur Fiedler and the Boston Pops. The
mayor of Boston, John B. Hines, was the
special guest that night.

Cancelled in 1957, the series was revived
four years later, without Fran Allison, in a
five-minute format, broadcast daily. The
program was titled *Burr Tillstrom's Kukla,
Fran and Ollie.* Fran was invited back for a
1969 Public Television revival, which lasted
two years. In 1975 the group appeared in a
syndicated half-hour format produced by
Tillstrom and Martin Tahse. The Kuklapolitan Players and Ms. Allison also hosted *The
CBS **Children's Film Festival,*** which
aired during the 1971/72 season.

## THE MAGIC COTTAGE

*Monday-Friday, 6:30–7:00 p.m.: Dumont*
*Debut: 7/18/49; Cancellation: 2/9/51*
*Producer: Hal Cooper*
*Hostess: Pat Meikle*

Set in a small cottage equipped with a drawing board, this story-telling series brought to
life characters from classic children's stories.
These included *Goldilocks* and *Jack and the
Beanstalk,* as well as contemporary stories.

Hostess Pat Meikle, an artist and accomplished actress, sketched a character who,
by animated sequences, would "leap off"
the drawingboard and participate in the
show with his mentor. Each character told a
story that would be left incomplete at the
close of the episode. This cliffhanger format
whetted the audience's appetite for the next
show.

Ms. Meikle and her husband, Hal
Cooper, launched *Dumont Kindergarten* in
1948, out of which grew *The TV Babysitter,*
which, in turn, developed into this show.
Meikle and Cooper brought one major
character through all three shows: Wilmer
the Pigeon. Cartoons included *Oogie the
Ogre's Christmas* and *Mr. Voice from
Nowhere,* the latter a disembodied voice,
complete with echo, which served as announcer. Games and contests provided par-

*Magic Cottage*: Pat Meikle. (Courtesy of Hal Cooper.)

ticipatory filler material.

*The Magic Cottage* was produced in front of a live audience at New York's Wanamaker Department Store in lower Manhattan. The store's upper level was the locale for the production of other shows, including **Captain Video** (1949–50).

Cooper and Meikle originally met while attending the University of Michigan. Cooper was a child actor on radio's *Rainbow House,* hosted by "Big Brother" Bob Emery. Since *Magic Cottage,* he has directed a number of successful series, including *The Dick Van Dyke Show, The Flying Nun, Gidget* and the daytime drama series, *Search for Tomorrow.* More recently he has produced *Love, Sidney* for NBC.

## MR. I MAGINATION

*Sunday, 7:00–7:30 p.m.: CBS*
*Debut: 5/29/49; Cancellation: 4/13/52*
*Producers: Norman and Irving Pincus, Worthington Miner*
*Creator: Paul Tripp*

*Cast: Paul Tripp, Ruth Enders, Ted Tiller, Joe Silver, Richard Boone*

*Meet Me, Mr. I Magination*
*The Man with the magic reputation.*
*Did I hear you wish to go*
*Where you think you cannot go?*
*Just ask me, Mr. I Magination*
*Can do whatever you*
*Would never dream that you could do*
*I'm quite a treasure*
*So it's a pleasure*
*To introduce to you*
*Just guess who*
*Mr. I Magination*
*The Man with the magic reputation.*

This musical refrain opened and closed each episode of this children's show, hosted by Paul Tripp. Tripp was known for his much-loved children's book, *Tubby, the Tuba* and various other stories. Mr. I Magination (Tripp) was a warm and gentle train

engineer dressed in overalls and cap. Each week he took his young "passengers" on a musical journey to the place of fables— *Imagination Land.*

The aim of the journey was to bring dreams to life. Tripp, "aboard" his railroad train, enjoined his audience to "act out" their imaginings. His philosophy was that anything was possible. Tripp created many of the imaginary situations in the show, but audience participation was encouraged. Scores of letters were received each week outlining the dreams viewers wished to see come true. A number were used on the show.

Mr. I Magination, always smiling, singing and wearing his bright yellow pants, took youngsters to such places as "Ambition Town," "Seaport City," and "I Wish I Were Land." Historical figures were personified by young actors, who interacted with the children.

Pianist Ray Carter composed and played the music for the series. He worked closely with Paul Tripp on the show's musical elements. Ruth Enders, leading lady and regular on the show, was in reality Tripp's wife. She played all the female roles, often as many as five per episode.

The idea for Mr. I Magination dates back to before World War II, when Tripp worked at a settlement house on New York City's Lower East Side. He contributed his time and energy to young kids in need of love and guidance, teaching them drama and helping them put on shows. When Paul's book, *Tubby, the Tuba* was published, it was brought to the attention of Norman and Irving Pincus. Inspired by "Tubby," the Pincuses approached Paul to assist them in developing a children's show. Thus, they became the show's producers.

The producers sold the concept to CBS, with assistance from Tripp's agent, Ted Ashley. Ashley founded an entertainment talent agency, Ashley Famous, which later became the world renowned International Creative Management (ICM). Ashley went on to become Chairman of Warner Com-

*Mr. I Magination* (left to right): Paul Tripp, Ted Tiller, Joe Silver, and Ruth Enders. (Courtesy of Paul Tripp.)

munications.

During Mr. I Magination's first 80 weeks, the program had no advertiser support. The network ran only public service announcements in place of commercials. Later, Nestle sponsored the show. Tripp worked closely with the food giant and assisted in the writing of its commercials. Problems later developed between the network and the sponsor, resulting in Nestle withdrawing its support. For six months in 1951, despite strong ratings, Mr. I Magination was silenced. Then, by massive popular demand, CBS returned the series to its schedule as a network-sustained item. During its lifetime *Mr. I Magination* won many honors, including the Look Award, the Peabody Award, the Ohio State University Award, the Variety Showmanship Award and an Emmy.

After this success, Paul Tripp hosted two local children's shows. He produced and starred in *On the Carousel* (1954–1959) and designed, wrote and starred in *Birthday House* (1963–1969). In addition to his series work, Tripp has had roles on stage, on television and in movies. His stage credits include *Othello, Will Rogers USA, 1776, Echoes, 49th Cousin, Temper the Wind, Jeremiah* and *Cyrano de Bergerac*. Roles in television series include *Perry Mason, The Barbara Stanwyck Show, The Defenders, Dobie Gillis* and *The Dick Van Dyke Show*. In addition, he portrayed the role of Thomas Edison in a Public Television special.

In 1946 animator George Pal made a "puppetoon" of Tubby the Tuba. Pal was responsible for such landmark motion science fiction films as *Destination Moon* and *War of the Worlds*. Tubby was also made into a theatrical short which received an Oscar nomination.

Whenever he is asked about *Mr. I Magination*, Tripp points out that the show encouraged young viewers to use their imaginations in creative ways. Consequently, there was little need for props, whose absence was dictated by the show's budget.

## THE QUIZ KIDS

*Wednesday, 8:00–8:30 p.m.: NBC*
*Saturday, 10:00–10:30 p.m.: CBS*
*Thursday, 10:30–11:00 p.m.: CBS*
*Debut: 3/1/49; Cancellation: 9/52 (NBC)*
*Return: 1/53; Cancellation: 11/53 (CBS)*
*Return: 1/56; Cancellation: 9/27/56 (CBS)*
*Producer: Rachael Stevenson*
*Hosts: Joe Kelly (1949–53), Clifton Fadiman (1956)*

This popular game show began life as a radio program in 1940. It made the transition to television in January, 1949, on local Chicago station WNBQ.

A panel of five bright youngsters, aged six to 16, competed against each other by answering questions posed by viewers. Each youngster was knowledgeable in a specific field. A child could remain with the show as long as he or she was successful.

One of the most famous child prodigies on the show was Robert Strom, an expert in astronomy, who remained with the show for close to six months. As he got older he branched out into physics and mathematics. Strom subsequently appeared on many other game shows and he won a substantial amount of money on *The $64,000 Question*.

Joe Kelly hosted the original radio version and the first four years of the television presentation. Ironically, he had a very limited education. He left school after the sixth grade.

An updated version of *The Quiz Kids* was syndicated in 1980, produced jointly by RKO General and Columbia Pictures Television. It mirrored the original format.

## THE SINGING LADY

*Sunday, 6:30–7:00 p.m.: ABC*
*Debut: 11/7/48; Cancellation: 8/6/50*

*The Singing Lady*: Irene Wicker.

**Producer:** *Blair Walliser*
**Writer/Performer:** *Ireene Wicker*

Just as she had on her long-running radio program broadcast nationally from 1930 through the mid 1970s, children's program award-winner Ireene Wicker wrote and told stories on *The Singing Lady*. In this television program, Ms. Wicker used the Suzari Marionettes to help her act out her stories, which included American Indian Legends, fairy tales, and childhood incidents in the lives of world and national leaders, composers, artists and writers. All of Ms. Wicker's stories were written in a style and on a level that held appeal to her audience, which ranged in age from five to eighty. Her stories emphasized the importance of courtesy and compassion, and avoided depicting any cruelty or violence.

In 1952, Ms. Wicker appeared as hostess of the Dumont network's *Little Lady Party*. In 1953, she returned to her previous format with *Ireene Wicker Story Time*.

Ms. Wicker was an early pioneer in television, having been chosen by Sir Cedric Harwicke to play Puck in his production of Shakespeare's *Midsummer-Night's Dream*, televised for internal viewing in Chicago before stationary cameras in 1932.

## SUPER CIRCUS

**Sunday:** *4:00 – 5:00 p.m.: ABC*
**Debut:** *1/16/49;* **Cancellation:** *6/3/56*
**Producer:** *Jack Gibney, Phil Patton*
**Hosts:** *Claude Kirchner, Jerry Colonna*

This 60-minute circus show was spawned from a Chicago radio quiz program. Claude Kirchner, producer Phil Patton and Harold Stokes conceived of the show as a kind of visual extravaganza, containing music and a variety of humorous skits in a "big top" format. Just about everything seen at a real circus appeared, at one time or another, on this imaginative show, including cyclists, trampoline artists, contests for audience participants and singing acts. But more than any other factor, the show's remarkable popularity was due to the beautiful, baton-twirling Mary Hartline. Her charm and good looks made her a topic of conversation throughout the nation. The slapstick antics of the three resident clowns—Cliffy Soblier, Sandy Dobritch and Nicky Francis—were also important in the success of the show.

When the show moved to New York in 1955, Kirchner and Hartline resigned. Jerry Colonna took over Kirchner's role, and Sandy Worth replaced Hartline.

# UNCLE MISTLETOE AND HIS ADVENTURES

*Monday—Friday,* 5:45—6:00 p.m.: ABC
*Debut:* 9/48; *Cancellation:* 12/21/52
*Producer:* Steve Hatos
*Hostess:* Jennifer Holt, Doris Larson
*Puppeteers:* The Marshall Field Marionette
    Company
*Voices:* Johnny Coons

Foot, Cone & Belding, the advertising agency for the Marshall Field department store in Chicago, was the catalyst for the creation of Uncle Mistletoe. The agency, assigned to create a figurehead character for the store's annual Christmas display, designed a non-sectarian "Father Christmas" resembling an English coachman.

Uncle Mistletoe, a 12-inch-high puppet, was featured in the store's windows, complete with a supporting cast. The character first appeared on television when the advertising agency arranged for Marshall Field to sponsor a local 15-minute children's program, broadcast on WENR. The popularity of the show led to its move to ABC's Chicago affiliate, WGN, and network exposure.

The puppet's human co-star was Jennifer Holt (later, Doris Larson). Uncle Mistletoe mingled with the inhabitants of Candy Cane Lane, a magical thoroughfare where dreams came true. His friends—all puppets—included Olio, Molio, Rolio, Aunt Judy, Skippy Monkey, Obediah Pig, Tony Pony and Humphrey Mouse.

Ray Chan wrote the programs. The puppets were created and operated by Marshall Field's own marionette company. Johnny Coons provided all the voices. Coons later went into partnership with Chan and Bill Newton to form CNC Productions. The company produced the popular **Uncle Johnny Coons** show, which was carried nationally by both CBS and NBC in 1954.

# VERSITILE VARIETIES JUNIOR EDITION

*Friday,* 9:30—10:00 p.m.: ABC
*Debut:* 9/51; *Cancellation:* 12/14/51
    (ABC)
*Supplier:* Basch Radio and T.V. Productions, Inc.
*Host:* Lady Iris Mountbatten
*Cast:* Eva Marie Saint, Edie Adams

This program derived from a TV commercial spokesperson, created for *Bonafide Mills,* a manufacturer of floor coverings. The charming character, "Bonnie Maid," originally portrayed by Anne Francis, became the focus of an adult variety show titled *Versatile Varieties.* In 1951 the series spawned a children's version, aptly named *Versatile Varieties Junior Edition.* Iris Mountbatten entertained a young live audience, recounting stories and enacting simple sketches.

*Versatile Varieties* (left to right): Carol Ohmart, Anne Francis, Eve Marie Saint. (Courtesy of Buddy Basch Feature Syndicate.)

1949-1950 Season

# THE BIG TOP

*Saturday, 12:00 – 1:00 p.m.: CBS*
*Debut: 7/1/50; Cancellation: 9/21/57*
*Producer: Charles Vanda*
*Ringmaster: Jack Sterling*
*Clowns: Ed McMahon, Chris Keegan*
*Regular performers: Circus Dan, the Muscle Man, Lott and Joe Anders, La Paloma*

*The Big Top* featured American and Foreign circus acts, many of which traveled from Europe to appear on the show.

This series aired for six months on CBS's prime-time schedule before being moved to Saturday mornings, where it continued for the next seven years. It was filmed in Camden, New Jersey, the winter home of many traveling circuses. One of the performers was the relatively unknown Ed McMahon. He was then working for CBS's Philadelphia radio affiliate, WCAU, writing, producing and hosting as many as 13 shows at once. Producer Charles Vanda had hoped to offer McMahon the role of ringmaster—the host of the show—but CBS insisted on Jack Sterling. McMahon instead became the principal clown—a more popular and appealing character. As he did in radio, McMahon wrote his own material. He remained in the medium as a pitchman for commercials until joining the inimitable *Tonight Show* as announcer and right-hand man for Johnny Carson.

# BILLY BOONE AND COUSIN KIB

*Sunday, 6:30 – 7:00 p.m.: CBS*
*Debut: 7/9/50; Cancellation: 8/27/50*
*Producer: Judy Dupuy*

Figures that "came to life" when sketched on camera were popular on children's shows during television's early years. Such was the case with Billy Boone and Cousin Kib.

Billy Boone was an animated figure created by cartoonist Carroll Colby, whose nickname was "Kib." Boone was presented in assorted daring cliffhanger adventures. The concept was extremely popular with young audiences, who couldn't wait for the next episode. The show's format was divided into games, sing-a-longs and an animated cartoon adventure. A small studio audience attended.

The series was a summer replacement for CBS's popular **Mr. I Magination** (1949/50).

# CACTUS JIM

*Monday – Friday, 6:00 – 6:30 p.m.: NBC*
*Debut: 10/31/49; Cancellation: 10/26/51*
*Producer: George Heinemann*
*Hosts: Clarence Hartzell (1949 – 1951), Bill Bailey (1951)*

This series showed Western movies, which were introduced by "Cactus Jim," a grizzled old-timer who looked and acted the part. The character was instrumental in the series' success. Also featured on the program was Clarence Hartzell's dog, which became a favorite with young viewers.

The show originated on Chicago's station WNBQ, where it was produced on a very small budget, to the distinct pleasure of station executives. It netted a substantial profit. Hartzell was an accomplished radio actor and TV host. He portrayed the part of "Uncle Fletcher" in the successful daytime radio series *Vic and Sade*. He also played the lead in *County Sheriff*.

*Cactus Jim*: Bill Bailey in the title role. (Courtesy of Bill Bailey.)

# CHILDREN'S SKETCH BOOK

*Saturday, 7:00–7:30 p.m.: NBC*
*Debut: 1/7/50; Cancellation: 2/4/50*
*Director: Barry Bernard*
*Storyteller: Edith Skinner*
*Illustrator: Lisl Weil*

Produced live, this short-lived series moved from daytime to prime time. Edith Skinner told stories in rhyme, accompanied by songs and drawings by Lisl Weil.

# CRASH CORRIGAN'S RANCH

*Saturday, 7:00–7:30 p.m.: ABC*
*Debut: 7/15/50; Cancellation: 9/29/50*
*Host: Ray Corrigan*

Ray "Crash" Corrigan, a star of low-budget Western movies, hosted this children's variety series. Made up of musical acts and sketches, most of which were performed by Country and Western singers and instrumentalists, it aired for only 11 weeks.

# LIFE WITH SNARKY PARKER

*Monday-Friday, 7:45–8:00 p.m.: CBS*
*Debut: 1/9/50; Cancellation: 8/30/50*
*Producer: Bil and Cora Baird*
*Director: Yul Brynner*
*Creators/Puppeteers: Bil and Cora Baird*

This series portrayed life in the Old West. Marionettes operated by the Bairds played the various characters.

*Snarky Parker* was deputy sheriff of Hot Rock, in love with the local school teacher and in constant conflict with Ronald Rodent, the town tough. Additional members of the cast were Slugger, the piano player at the Bent Elbow Saloon, and Paw, the schoolteacher's father. There were 15 principals in the series, and other puppets appeared in supporting roles.

In August, 1950, Snarky Parker rode his horse Heathcliffe into a new late afternoon

television slot, in a weekday series. He maintained law and order for about a month before his final ride into the sunset.

Bil Baird was already an accomplished entertainer at the time of the show's debut. Before moving into television, he had performed in night clubs with Snarky, a

character he had created in the 1940s. When the TV series left the air, Baird took the puppet back on the club circuit. After *Snarky Parker*, the Bairds created and staged other series for television, including *The Whistling Wizard*, comprised mostly of the characters from *Life with Snarky Parker*.

Cora Baird died in 1967, but Bil remains active with his own company, producing industrial films and staging puppet shows for commercials. Director Yul Brynner later shaved his head and became famous for his portrayal of the king of Siam in the musical, *The King and I*.

*Life With Snarky Parker*: The assembled cast. (Courtesy of Bil Baird.)

# MAGIC SLATE

*Friday, 8:00–8:30 p.m.: NBC*
*Debut: 6/2/50; Cancellation: 8/25/50*
*Producer: Norman Gant*

This series dramatized both classic and contemporary children's stories. It was produced under the supervision of both Norman Gant and Charlotte Chorpenning of the Goodman Children's Theater in Chicago. *Magic Slate* alternated with the highly successful **The Quiz Kids** (1948/49), which also originated in the Windy City. *Magic Slate* returned briefly in the summer of 1951 as a Sunday afternoon show.

# THE MAGIC CLOWN

*Sunday, 11:30–11:45 a.m.; NBC*
*Debut: 9/11/49; Cancellation: 6/27/54*
*Producer: Al Garry*
*Host: Zovella, the Magic Clown*

Zovella the Clown was the magician/host of this 15-minute "fill-in" series, comprised of games, songs and magic set in a circus background. Children from the audience performed singing commercials for the show's sponsor, Bonomo, and assisted Zovella with his tricks.

# SLEEPY JOE

*Monday-Friday, 6:45–7:00 p.m.: ABC*
*Debut: 10/3/49; Cancellation: 10/28/49*
*Creator: Jimmy Scribner*
*Puppeteer: Velma Dawson*
*Voices: Jimmy Scribner*

Jimmy Scribner, linguist and student of dialects, originally created this show for ABC radio. Scribner portrayed "Sleepy Joe," an elderly, wizened storyteller of colorful tales. His audience was young Gayle, Jimmy's real-life daughter. The switch to television was made on local station KTSL in Los Angeles. The network series was revised and

formatted as a filmed puppet show. In 1951 a full-color adaptation went into syndication.

# SMILIN' ED'S GANG

*Saturday, 6:30–7:00 p.m.: NBC*
*Debut: 8/26/50; Cancellation: 5/19/51 (NBC)*
*Return: 10:30–11:00 a.m., 8/11/51; Cancellation: 4/11/53 (ABC)*
*Return: 10:30–11:00 a.m., 8/22/53; Cancellation: 4/16/55 (NBC)*
*Producer: Frank Ferrin*
*Host: Ed McConnell*

*Cast*

Gunga Ram . . . . . . . . . . . . . .Nino Marcel
Rama . . . . . . . . . . . . . . . . . .Vito Scotti
The Maharajah . . . . . . . . . . .Lou Krugman
Shortfellow, the Poet . . . . .Alan Reed
The Teacher . . . . . . . . . . . . .Billy Gilbert
Buster Brown . . . . . . . . . . .Jerry Marin

*Voices*

Froggy, the Gremlin . . . . . . .Ed McConnell
Tige, the dog . . . . . . . . . . . . .Bud Tollefson
Midnight, the cat . . . . . . . . . .June Foray
Old Grandie . . . . . . . . . . . . .June Foray
Other performers: Joe Mazzuca, Peter Coo, Billy Race, Paul Cavanaugh

This children's series, hosted by Smilin' Ed McConnell and sponsored by Buster Brown shoes, was a TV version of McConnell's radio program, which had the same sponsor. McConnell played the piano, sang and read from his storybook, an activity for which he was famous. Every story, of course, had a moral. Also on the show was a diverse collection of whimsical animals and animate objects (including Grandie, a talking piano), providing humorous and musical interludes between storytelling. The show also featured filmed segments, including a costume drama titled *Gunga, the East India Boy*, a story set in India in the village of Bakore. Gunga Ram and his friend Rama regularly embarked on dangerous missions for their leader, the Maharajah.

The series carried a host of titles during its successful run on three of the networks. On NBC prime time, it was called *Smilin' Ed McConnell and his Buster Brown Gang,* a title it retained after being transferred a year later to Saturday mornings on CBS. There it ran for two more years: 1951 to 1953. Late in 1953 it moved to ABC for two more seasons, billed as *Smilin' Ed's Gang.* McConnell, already an elderly man when he began hosting the show, died in 1954. He was replaced by Andy Devine as host, and the series became *Andy's Gang.* In 1955 the show returned to NBC under this title, with the format and characters otherwise unchanged. Buster Brown, now the Brown Group, Inc., remained the sponsor and Frank Ferrin the producer.

Although produced on an extremely small budget, the series was a tremendous success. Buster Brown's appealing trademark, a boy and his canine companion named Tige, were made to order for television, where there is ample opportunity to exploit the visual identification of product.

Tige's voice was supplied by Bud Tollefson and Buster, his master, by Jerry Marin. These actors (and their voices) have worked extensively in television, radio and print commercials.

*Smilin' Ed's Gang*: Ed McConnell with Froggy and Midnight. (Courtesy of Brown Group, Inc.)

1950 - 1951 Season

# COWBOYS AND INJUNS

*Sunday, 6:00 – 6:30 p.m.: ABC*
*Debut: 10/15/50; Cancellation: 12/31/50*
*Host: Rex Bell*

This briefly aired show depicted historically accurate cowboy and Indian folklore against the backdrop of an outdoor corral and a tribal village. Prior to this network exposure, the show ran on station KECA (ABC) in Los Angeles.

# FASHION MAGIC

*Saturday, 11:00 – 11:30 a.m.: CBS*
*Debut: 11/10/50; Cancellation: 6/15/51*
*Producer: Robert Mayberry*
*Hostesses: Ilka Chase, Arlene Francis*

This program, aimed principally at the adolescent girl, provided information on beauty and fashion. The hostesses interviewed dress designers, cosmeticians, skin specialists, and the like.

# KID GLOVES

*Saturday, 7:30 – 8:00 p.m.: CBS*
*Debut: 2/24/51; Cancellation: 8/4/51*
*Producer/Director: Alan Bergman*
*Regulars: Frank Goodman, Bill Sears, John De Grosa*

This series featured extremely young boxers—aged three to 12—who competed in three-round contests of ten seconds each. The fights were refereed by Frank Goodman, who was both matchmaker and judge. Bill Sears was ringside correspondent. John De Grosa of the Pennsylvania State Athletic Commission interviewed celebrities from the world of sports between rounds and engaged in question and answer sessions with the audience. *Kid Gloves* started as a local Philadelphia program on WCAU before moving to the CBS network evening schedule.

# THE PAUL WINCHELL AND JERRY MAHONEY SPIEDEL SHOW

*Monday, 8:00 – 8:30 p.m.: NBC*
*Debut: 9/18/50; Cancellation: 5/23/54*
*Producer: Will Cowan*
*Master of Ceremonies: Paul Winchell*

*Regulars: Jerry Mahoney, Knucklehead Smith, Oswald, Dorothy Claire (1951– 52), Diane Sinclair and Ken Spaulding (1951–53), Mary Ellen Terry (1953– 54), Margaret Hamilton (1953–54), Maybin Hewe, Hilda Vaughn, Jimmy Blaine, Patricia Bright, Sid Raymond, The John Gart Orchestra*

Ventriloquist Paul Winchell and his dummies Jerry Mahoney, Knucklehead Smith and Oswald hosted this prime-time variety show, which mixed comedy, music and quizzes with a sprinkling of drama. Guest stars included Angela Lansbury, Robert Preston and Carol Burnett, the latter in one of her earliest television appearances.

A number of formats were used during the series' four-year run. Initially, there was a comedy routine on the program, titled "What's My Name?" A show with that name had been on radio, where questions alluding to a well-known individual would be put to a panel. On the television show, guest actors and actresses would act out clues to assist participants in identifying the celebrity. Contestants were taken from the studio audience, and viewers were invited to participate by phone.

In the variety segment, Winchell and his companions, Jerry, Knucklehead and Oswald, were accompanied by singer Dorothy Claire and dancers Diane Sinclair and Ken Spaulding. In the fall of 1953, a filmed dramatic vignette approximately ten minutes in length was added, featuring a well-known actor or actress in a minidrama, with Winchell in a supporting role. This insertion was dropped when the show returned to a comedy variety format for the remainder of its run.

Spiedel, manufacturer of wristwatch bands, sponsored the series. Winchell went from here to another NBC series, **Jerry Mahoney's Clubhouse** (1954/55), on Saturday mornings.

## ROOTIE KAZOOTIE

*Monday-Friday, 6:00–6:15 p.m.: NBC*
*Saturday, 11:00–11:30 a.m.: ABC*
*Debut: 12/9/50; Cancellation: 11/1/52*
*Return: 12/22/52; Cancellation: 5/7/54*
*Producer/Writer: Steve Carlin*
*Host: Todd Russell*

*Voices*

Rootie Kazootie . . . . . . . . . . .*Naomi Lewis*
El Squeako . . . . . . . . . . . . . .*Naomi Lewis*
Polka Dottie . . . . . . . . . . . . .*Naomi Lewis*
Poison Zoomack . . . . . . . . . .*Frank Milano*
Gala Poochie . . . . . . . . . . . .*Frank Milano*
Deetle Dootle . . . . . . . . . . . .*John Vee*

*Puppeteers: Paul Ashley and Frank Milano*

*Theme Song*
*Who is the boy who is full of zip and joy?*
*He's Rootie Kazootie:*
*Who is the lad who makes you feel so glad?*
*He's Rootie Kazootie:*
*I'm the leader of the Rootie-Kazootie Club and with me, there is (Arf! Arf!), Gala Poochie, the pup!*
*Let's all hear a Rootin' Kazootin' Cheer, For Rootie Kazootie!*

Here was the puppet personification of the "Little Leaguer," rooting and tooting on his kazoo; the program's initial airing as a local New York show was as *Rootie Tootie*, until a candy bar forced the name change. Rootie, with his baseball cap at a rakish angle, was accompanied by his faithful mutt, Gala Poochie, and the love of his young life, Polka Dottie. His arch-enemy and constant antagonist was Poison Zoomack.

There were two humans on the show, including its host, Todd Russell (Big Todd), and John Vee, who played Deetle Dootle.

The latter was a mute officer of the law, who used his extraordinary talents as a magician and mime artist to communicate without speech. Language, however, was important to the show. A fundamental element was the Rootie-Kazootie dialog, a sort of pig Latin that added a "Rootie" suffix to words. Music was also an integral part of the series, much of it composed by Milton Kaye, who also played the organ.

Each story was spun out to five episodes, beginning on Friday and running to the following Thursday. A parallel half-hour Saturday morning edition would focus on a different plot. It included the "Quiz-A-Rootie," in which youngsters from the audience answered simple questions on history and geography.

Over the years a number of sponsors underwrote the series, including RCA, the parent company of NBC, Coca Cola, Powerhouse Candy and Silvercup Bread.

## SANDY DREAMS

*Saturday, 7:00–7:30 p.m.: ABC*
*Debut: 10/7/50; Cancellation: 12/2/50*
*Producer: Bud Stefan*
*Host: Rose-Mary Iannone*

When Sandy, an eight-year-old girl, closed her eyes, she took the audience on journeys through her dreams. This musical fantasy series consisted of sketches, songs and choreography performed by alternating groups of young actors from the Los Angeles area. The program began as a local show in Los Angeles on KTLA before moving to the ABC network.

## SANDY STRONG

*Monday-Friday, 6:15–6:30 p.m.: ABC*
*Debut: 9/25/50; Cancellation: 3/23/51*
*Producer: George Anderson*

*Cast*
Mr. Mack . . . . . . .*Ray Suber (1950),*

*Forrest Lewis (1950 – 51)*

This daily series featured both actors and puppets in running stories that concluded on Fridays. Produced in Chicago, the series was considered expensive for its time. Its budget of between $25,000 and $30,000 per episode was necessary for the lavish sets and staging.

George Anderson, who wrote and produced the show, named his juvenile puppet lead "Sandy Strong" to perpetuate a strong, healthy image for the show's sponsor, Ovaltine. Anderson went on to produce **Magic Ranch** (1961/62), which also originated in Chicago. He still lives in the Windy City, where he writes books on magic and uses his skills as an illusionist to make sales presentations.

*Space Patrol*: Ed Kemmer—Commander Buzz Corey of the Space Patrol. (Courtesy of Ed Kemmer.)

# SPACE PATROL

*Saturday, 6:00 – 6:30 p.m.: ABC*
*Debut: 9/11/50; Cancellation: 2/26/55*
*Producers: Mike Mosser, Mike Devery,*
   *Helen Mosser*
*Creator: Mike Mosser*

## Cast

Commander Buzz Corey .Ed Kemmer
Cadet Happy . . . . . . . . . .Lyn Osborn
Carol Karlyle . . . . . . . . . .Virginia Hewitt
Dr. Von Meter . . . . . . . . .Rudolph Anders
Tonga . . . . . . . . . . . . . . . .Nina Bara
Announcer . . . . . . . . . . . .Jack Narz
Mr. Proteus . . . . . . . . . . .Marvin Miller
Prince Baccarratti
   (The Black Falcon) . . . .Bella Kovacs
Major Robbie Robertson .Ken Mayer
Secretary General
   of the United Planets . .Norman Jolley

Originally a local show in Los Angeles, this series went national in 1950. During its lifetime it was programmed as both a 15-minute and a 30-minute series, airing in various weekend time slots. Led by Commander Buzz Corey, The Space Patrol was an Earth-based security force charged with the protection of the United Planets, consisting of Earth, Mercury, Venus, Mars and Jupiter. The cast included Cadet Happy, Corey's youthful co-pilot; Carol, a *femme fatale* and daughter of the Secretary General, who has romantic feelings for the manly commander; Tonga, a beautiful but evil villain who eventually repents; and Dr. Von Meter, a scientist working for Space Patrol. Corey's problems revolve principally around the villainous activities of Mr. Proteus and Prince Baccarratti, alias the Black Falcon.

Set in the twenty-first century, episodes concerned the Space Patrol's continuing celestial battle against the forces of evil. Despite the action, no one was ever killed (the ultimate punishment was a blast from Corey's paralyzer gun). Time travel stories and imaginative space gadgetry were elements that helped make this series popular

during the 1950s, the period of space travel's infancy.

Marvin Miller (Mr. Proteus), later seen in the prime-time adult series *The Millionaire*, has provided voice-overs for many Saturday cartoons.

# TOM CORBETT, SPACE CADET

*Saturday: CBS*
*Debut: 10/2/50; Cancellation: 12/29/50*
   *CBS*
*Return: 1/1/51; Cancellation: 9/26/52*
   *ABC*
*Return: 7/7/51; Cancellation: 9/8/51*
   *NBC*
*Return: 8/29/53; Cancellation: 5/22/54*

*Dumont*
**Return:** *12/11/54;* **Cancellation:** *6/25/55*
NBC
**Producers:** *Stanley Wolfe, Al Ducovny,*
*Leonard Carlton*
**Supplier:** *Rockhill Productions*

### Cast

Tom Corbett . . . . . . . . . .*Frankie Thomas*
Capt. Strong (1950) . . . .*Michael Harvey*
Capt. Strong
   (1951–1952) . . . . . . . *Edward Bryce*
Astro, the Venusian  . . . .*Al Markim*
Roger Manning . . . . . . . .*Jan Merlin*
Dr. Joan Dale  . . . . . . . .*Margaret Garland*
Commander
   T. J. Fissell . . . . . . . . . .*Jack Grimes*

Based on the Robert A. Heinlein novel, *Space Cadet,* this science fiction series was set in the year 2350 A.D., at Space Academy, U.S.A. The academy trained young men and women to become Solar Guards, agents of a celestial police force enjoined to protect Earth, Jupiter, Mars and Venus. The planets were known collectively as the Solar Alliance. The program was CBS's answer to the rival Dumont network's highly successful series of 1948, *Captain Video,* which spawned a number of larger budgeted and more sophisticated science fantasy series.

*Tom Corbett* was notable for its scientific authenticity. Willie Ley, a popular scientist of the day, was engaged as a technical advisor, and suggested scientific subjects that could be explored within the framework of the program. Episodes pitted Corbett and his colleagues against such natural phenomena as dangerous gas fields, meteoric eruptions and weightlessness. Ray guns and cardboard villains were conspicuously absent. The special effects were a milestone in television animation.

Extremely popular, the show aired on each of the four networks. For much of 1951, it was carried by two of them simultaneously. During its five-year run, many future stars made guest appearances, including Jack Lord, Jack Klugman, and Jack Weston, famous, respectively, for *Hawaii 5-0, Quincy* and *Rod Brown, Rocket Ranger.*

*Tom Corbett—Space Cadet*: A scene from outer space. (Courtesy of Stanley Wolf.)

# THE TELECOMICS

*Monday – Friday,* 5:00 – 5:15 p.m.: NBC
*Debut: 9/18/50; Cancellation: 3/30/51*
*Supplier: Vallee Video*

This series, also known as *The NBC Comics,*
featured the first cartoons made especially
for the small screen. Among these were:
*Brother Goose, Joey and Jug, Rick Rack,
Special Agent* and *Sa-Lih. The Telecomics*
originated as a syndicated series in 1949.
When NBC picked it up in 1950 they introduced several new cartoons: *Danny March,
Johnny and Mr. Do-Right, Kid Champion*
and *Space Barton.*

Danny March was set in Metro City,
where Danny's parents were killed in an au-
tomobile accident. He was sent to live with
his somewhat disreputable uncle, who also
died a cruel death. Danny subsequently
grew up in an orphanage as a tough, self-
reliant youngster. Growing up on the street,
Danny witnessed the ease with which kids
took to crime, and he vowed to attempt to
stem that flood. Having failed to meet the
height requirements of the city police, he
devoted all his energies to becoming a
superlative private detective. His career
culminated in his becoming the Mayor's personal detective.

*Johnny and Mr. Do-Right* was the story
of the adventures of a young boy and his
dog.

*Kid Champion* centered on Eddie Hale,
whose dreams of becoming a musician were
set aside in deference to his father's wish
that he train as a prizefighter. His father was
a famous boxer who had only a year to live.
One day Eddie found himself the witness to
a robbery at a gas station. After participating
in the apprehension of the culprit, he as-
sumed the name "Kid Champion." Lucky
Skinner, a fight manager, persuaded Eddie
to turn professional. (Elements of the famous *Rocky* movies come to mind.) Episodes
described Eddie's long and arduous journey
to the top of the fight world.

In *Space Barton,* viewers were treated to
the adventures of Horace Barton, Jr., a
young man whose modest goal was to become nothing less than the greatest pilot in
the world. After graduating from college,
Horace joined the Army Air Corps and
tested the first U.S. jet, among other things.

# MR. WIZARD

*Saturday,* 12:30 – 1:00 p.m.: NBC
*Debut: 3/5/51; Cancellation: 9/5/65*
*Return: 9/11/71; Cancellation: 9/2/72*
*Producer: Jules Pewowar*
*Host: Don Herbert*

*Assistants: Bruce Lindgren, Rita Mac-
Laughlin, Alan Howard, Buzzy Podwell,
Betty Sue Albert*

Although it never received true commercial
advertising support, this show proved to be
one of television's most successful educational programs.

In 1951 Don Herbert, a radio actor and
one-time director of the Community Fund of
Chicago, brought the "Mr Wizard" idea to
producer Jules Pewowar at NBC's Chicago
station. Mr. Wizard, impersonated by Don
Herbert, provided visually dramatic demonstrations of simple scientific principles, all of
which were presented within the context of a
child's experience. Herbert often used
household objects to simplify the experi-
ments.

Until 1953, Mr. Wizard employed as his
assistant his 11-year old Chicago neighbor,
Willy. From then on he alternated a girl and
a boy. When the show moved to New York,
Pewowar relinquished his role as producer
to Herbert and went on to produce PBS's
*Over Easy.* Although at one time partially
sponsored by The Cereal Institute, *Mr.
Wizard* was always produced on a limited
budget and aired by NBC as a non-profit
public affairs program. The show won many
awards, including two Thomas Alva Edison
Foundation National Mass Media Awards
(1961 and 1963) and two Emmy nomina-

*Mr. Wizard*: Don Herbert in the title role. (Courtesy of Don Herbert.)

tions (1960 and 1963). By 1954, only three years into its uninterrupted 14-year run, the show had spawned more than 5,000 *Mr.* *Wizard* science clubs across the United States and Canada, with a membership in excess of 100,000.

# 1951-1952 Season

# FOODINI, THE GREAT

*Monday-Friday, 6:30 – 6:45 p.m.: ABC*
*Debut: 8/23/51; Cancellation: 12/29/51*
*Producers: Hope and Morey Bunin*
*Hosts: Ellen Parker and Lou Prentis*

First seen on CBS's **Lucky Pup** (1947/ 48), Foodini, a magician with a propensity for the black arts, and Pinhead, his dimwitted assistant, starred in this puppet show. Puppeteers Morey and Hope Bunin, creators of Lucky Pup and Jolo the clown, produced and directed this spin-off. Episodes were told in a story-book format, with equal helpings of adventure, comedy and suspense. The two characters created nasty problems for whoever was unlucky enough to cross their path.

The show garnered strong ratings and secured major sponsorship from such companies as Bristol-Myers and Sundial Shoes. The national magazines *Time* and *Redbook* paid tribute to the Bunins' talents, further enhancing the show's standing. As puppeteers the Bunins were extraordinary. Their technique combined the mobility of marionettes with the direct manipulation of hand puppets.

*Foodini the Great*: Pinhead and Foodini. (Courtesy of Morey Bunin.)

# FEARLESS FOSDICK

*Sunday,* 6:30 – 7:00 p.m.: NBC
*Debut:* 7/20/52; *Cancellation:* 9/28/52
*Producer:* Charles Buggenheim
*Creator:* Al Capp

*Voices and Puppets:* The Mary Chase Marionette Company

This series was derived from Al Capp's famous comic strip, *Li'l Abner.* Both animation and puppets were used to depict the humor-

*Fearless Fosdick*: Fearless Fosdick taking a beating. (Courtesy of Pantomime Pictures Group.)

ous escapades of Fearless Fosdick, a parody of Chester Gould's *Dick Tracy*.

Fosdick was Li'l Abner's favorite bumbling detective. He meant well and tried his best to be effective, but he was frequently subjected to abuse from the police department, and received little or no reward for his efforts. Despite these obstacles, Fosdick's magnanimous character shined through, as he doggedly pursued those who violated the law.

Fosdick appeared to be impervious to pain. He took even more abuse from those he tried to put behind bars than he did from his fellow detectives. (He was frequently used for target practice by hoodlums, who pumped him with bullets. The lead appeared to pass right through him.)

This series premiered as a Sunday afternoon program, but within a month it moved to prime-time. Al Capp's original characters had been syndicated in hundreds of newspapers around the world, as well as appearing in comic books and cloth and paperback books. Capp died in November 1979, shortly after discontinuing *Li'l Abner*.

## HAIL THE CHAMP!

*Saturday, 6:30 – 7:00 p.m.: ABC*
*Debut: 9/22/51; Cancellation: 6/14/52*
*Return: 12/27/52; Cancellation: 6/13/53*
*Producer: Herb Allen*
*Hosts: Herb Allen, Howard Roberts, Angel*
  *Casey*

Six youngsters chosen from the studio audience competed against each other for the title of "The Champ." The contests were athletic in nature and bore a resemblance to juvenile Olympic games. Each episode featured three qualifying rounds in which a boy competed against a girl. The three finalists completed a timed course of activities, and the Champ received a prize, often a bicycle.

Originating from Chicago, this show was first seen on prime-time before moving to Saturday mornings. Chuckles candy was the sponsor.

## KIDS AND COMPANY

*Saturday, 11:00 – 11:30 a.m.: Dumont*
*Debut: 9/1/51; Cancellation: 5/2/53*
*Producer: Wyatt-Schuebell Productions*
*Hosts: Johnny Olsen, Ham Fisher*

This children's variety show, hosted by Johnny Olsen and Ham Fisher, was an "opportunity knocks" showcase for talented youngsters.

The most important feature of the series was the segment, "Kid of the Week," in which the National Junior Chamber of Commerce honored children who had demonstrated great courage and determination. The recipient was flown to the show and presented with his or her award on the air. Many talented children performed on the show, including George Segal, Leslie Uggams, Bobby Darin, and Marvin Hamlisch, all of whom grew up to be stars of the entertainment world. Guest celebrities presented the awards on behalf of the program's sponsor, St. Louis' International Shoe Company.

In addition to this Dumont series, Johnny Olsen hosted *Johnny Olsen's Rumpus Room* five days a week and was also master of ceremonies on *Star Time*. Co-host Ham Fisher was the creator of *Joe Palooka*, the famous comic-strip and comic-book character.

## ONCE UPON A FENCE

*Sunday, 6:30 – 7:00 p.m.: NBC*
*Debut: 4/13/52; Cancellation: 7/20/52*

This briefly seen live-action series told stories with musical accompaniment.

Dave Kaigler sang and played guitar, while Katherine Heger, "Princess Katherine of Storyland," unravelled the magical threads of her stories.

Heger portrayed many characters in the stories. The program originated in Philadelphia.

*Kids and Co.*: Johnny Olsen. (Courtesy of Johnny Olsen.)

*Sky King*: Gloria Winters with the Songbird. (Courtesy of Gloria Winters.)

## SKY KING

**Alternate Sundays,** *5:30–6:00 p.m.:* NBC
**Alternate Saturdays,** *11:30–12:00 noon:* ABC
**Saturday,** *12:00–12:30 p.m.:* CBS
**Debut:** *9/51;* **Cancellation:** *10/52 (NBC)*
**Return:** *11/52;* **Cancellation:** *9/54 (ABC)*
**Return:** *10/59;* **Cancellation:** *9/66 (CBS)*
**Producers:** *Jack Chertok, Al McGowan*

### Cast

Skylar King . . . . . . . . . . . . . *Kirby Grant*
Penny King . . . . . . . . . . . . . *Gloria Winters*
Clipper King . . . . . . . . . . . . *Ron Hagerthy*
The Sheriff . . . . . . . . . . . . . *Ewing Mitchell*

Skylar King, known as "Sky" to his friends, was an Arizona rancher and pilot. His spread the "Flying Crown Ranch" was so large that rather than conventionally police it on horseback, he traveled in a twin-engined Cessna known as *The Songbird.*

The program originated on radio, where it ran from 1946 until 1954. In 1951 Paul Harper and Jack Pittman of the advertising agency of Needham, Harper and Steers persuaded Jack Chertok to take on the task of adapting the show to television. The talented producer established the format and after two years handed the reins to Al McGowan. Much of the action took place on the ground, but to live up to the show's title, approximately six minutes of each 30 minute episode consisted of matched black and white aerial footage. These scenes were the responsibility of Paul Mantz, an aviator, instructor and one-time advisor to the woman pilot Amelia Earhart.

*Sky King:* Gloria Winters and Kirby Grant. (Courtesy of Gloria Winters.)

This show originally transmitted locally from Philadelphia on WCAU.

## THE WHISTLING WIZARD

*Saturday, 11:00–11:30 a.m.: CBS*
*Debut: 11/3/51; Cancellation: 9/20/52*
*Producer: Bil Baird*
*Puppetry and Voices: Bil and Cora Baird*
*Writer: Allan Stern*

Bil and Cora Baird's delightful puppets were the players in this droll fantasy series. The setting was "The Land of Beyond," a magical world inhabited principally by puppets from the Baird's previous series, *Life with Snarky Parker*.

Bright as a button, young hero "J.P." was fashioned by Baird after the son of a close friend. His constant companion was the inimitable horse Heathcliffe, the most popular character in *Snarky Parker*. Both were watched over by Dooley, a leprechaun with a magic flute, otherwise known as "The Whistling Wizard."

The villains were Kohlrabi and his monstrous mistress the Spider Lady, who conjured up powerful black magic with the cry "Elia Kazan!" Other puppet characters included J. Fiddler Crab, Davy Jones, an old sea salt, and the team of Flannel Mouse and Charlemane, a long-maned lion. Flannel idled the time away on his "mouse-organ," and with one eye watched over his loyal but not very bright friend Charlemane. The Land of Beyond was inhabited by other good and not-so-good characters, including mermaids and dragons.

The point of the series was to educate the young audience in the "ups and downs" of life, and to demonstrate that perseverance is fundamental to success.

*The Whistling Wizard:* Captain Davy Jones. (Courtesy of Bil Baird.)

## WHAT IN THE WORLD?

*Saturday, 10:00–10:30 a.m.: CBS*
*Debut: 10/7/51; Cancellation: 4/2/55*
*Producer: Robert A. Forrest*
*Host: Dr. Froelich Rainey*

This question-and-answer show featured panelists from the fields of history, archaeology and anthropology. Individual artifacts and photographs of sections of larger pieces were identified by such regulars as Dr. Carlton Coon and Dr. Alfred Kidder. Each correct response was scored according to the complexity of the question.

*The Whistling Wizard*: "J.P." with Bil and Cora Baird. (Courtesy of Bil Baird.)

# 1952-1953 Season

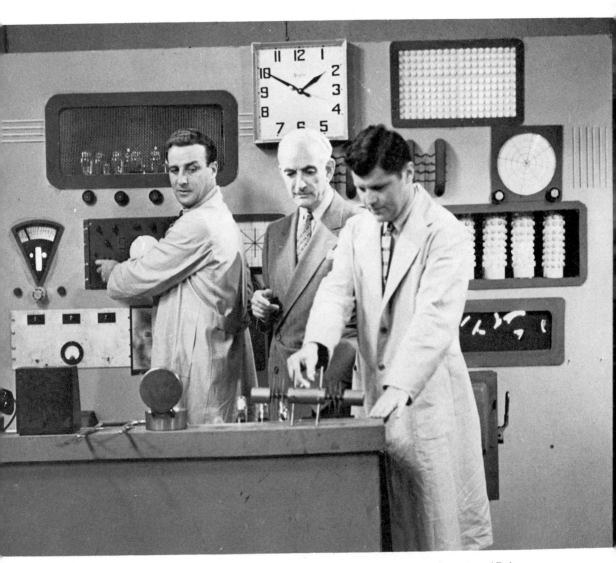

*Atom Squad* (left to right): Bob Courtleigh, Bram Nossem, and Bob Hastings. (Courtesy of Bob Courtleigh.)

## ATOM SQUAD

*Monday–Friday, 5:00 – 5:15 p.m.: NBC*
*Debut: 7/6/53; Cancellation: 1/22/54*
*Executive Producer: Adrien Samish*

Steve Elliot . . . . . . . . . . . . . *Bob Coutleigh*
Dave, Steve's assistant . . . . *Bob Hastings*
Chief, Steve's superior . . . . *Bram Nossem*

This science fiction series aired at the height of the McCarthy Era and its Communist witch hunts. The political climate of the time was reflected in such episodes as *The Five Steps to the Kremlin* and *The Ships that Sailed Nowhere*.

Operating from their secret headquarters in Manhattan, Steve Elliot and his cohorts battled all manner of evils below, above and on the ground, while protecting America's atomic secrets.

Paul Monash wrote many episodes for this series, which was produced by NBC "in-house." Monash went on to produce *Butch Cassidy and The Sundance Kid*, *Slaughterhouse Five* and *Carrie* for the big screen. His television credits include *Peyton Place* and *Judd For The Defense*. Bob Hastings (brother of Don, *Captain Video's* Video Ranger) has been seen in many television series, including *All In The Family*, *McHale's Navy*, and, presently, *General Hospital*.

# THE DING DONG SCHOOL

**Monday-Friday, 9:00 – 9:30 a.m.: NBC**
**Debut:** 11/24/52; **Cancellation:** 12/28/56
**Executive Producer:** Henry Sapperstein
**Producer:** Reinald Werrenrath
**Hostess:** Dr. Frances Horwich

This educational series, one of the first of its kind, was aimed at the pre-school child.

Dr. Frances Horwich, the hostess and mediator, was known on the show as "Miss Frances." She conducted lessons in such activities as finger-painting and singing.

At this time, vociferous critics began to lay crime, violence, and a deterioration in language skills at television's door. Dr. Horwich headed the watchdog "Children's Program Review Committee," convened by NBC in an attempt to keep the network's house in order. Her erudition was beyond reproach. Prior to the series, Dr. Horwich had been Head of the Education Department at Roosevelt College (now Roosevelt University) in Chicago.

The program initially aired on station WMAQ in Chicago, and its success brought it to the NBC network. After four years

and changing mores, sponsors began slipping away, and NBC cancelled the show. Dr. Horwich owned the rights to the series, and she took it into syndication in 1959, in New York and Los Angeles. The series found its title when the infant daughter of the producer noticed a hand ringing a bell in the opening sequence of the test broadcast. Dr. Horwich's opening rhyme was: "I'm your schoolbell, ding dong ding/Boys and girls all hear me ring." The show's two principle sponsors were Scott Paper Towels and General Mills.

# JOHNNY JUPITER

**Saturday, 7:30 – 8:00 p.m.: Dumont**
**Saturday, 5:30 – 6:00 p.m.: ABC**
**Debut:** 3/21/53; **Cancellation:** 6/13/53
**Return:** 9/5/53; **Cancellation:** 5/29/54 (ABC)
**Cast:** Vaughn Taylor, Gilbert Mack (Dumont); Wright King, Cliff Hall, Pat Peardon (ABC)
**Puppeteer:** Carl Harms (Dumont)
**Voices:** Gilbert Mack (Dumont)

This series took a satirical look at our civilization as seen through the eyes of the inhabitants of the planet Jupiter.

Ernest P. Duckweather was the janitor of a television station who liked to play with studio equipment. One evening he accidentally made contact with two beings from outer space: Johnny Jupiter and his associate "B-12" (both were actually glove puppets). Johnny and Duckweather conversed via their respective TV screens, and a friendship of sorts developed. Johnny was very interested in the human race and its habits, having picked up television programs from Earth. He therefore knew a little about life on this planet, and he and his fellow Jupiterians were bewildered. Duckweather would attempt to explain why we do the silly things we do, and he often had difficulty answering. As a result, Duckweather became a celebrity on Jupiterian television.

*Johnny Jupiter* was a show made to order for the Dumont network; it appealed to the entire family. Its challenging and amusing format was conceived by Martin Stone, a former executive producer of *Howdy Doody,* and Jerry Coopersmith. The show won the praise of viewers and critics alike.

As with most children's shows of the period, advertising support was minimal and the budgets were small. This was why all the Jupiterians, apart from Johnny, had the same faces.

In September of 1953 ABC made some cast changes, and a new character, Mr. Frisbee, owner of the Frisbee General Store, was introduced. Duckweather became a store clerk whose hobby of tinkering with electronic gadgetry brought him face to face with Johnny Jupiter (on television). The series continued to parody the behavior of Earth's inhabitants: in one episode Jupiterian children were punished for spending too much time reading books; they were forced to watch television.

## LASH OF THE WEST

*Sunday, 6:30–6:45 p.m.: ABC*
*Debut: 1/4/53; Cancellation: 4/26/53*
*Producer: Howco International*

Cowboy movie star Lash LaRue hosted this briefly aired series. He demonstrated the tricks and stunts he had performed in Western films of the 1940s. LaRue was known for his bullwhip and dazzling daredevil manner.

*Lash of the West*: The cast on the set. (Courtesy of Filmation Associates)

*Lash of the West*: Lash LaRue getting the worst of it. (Courtesy of Filmation Associates.)

## MEET ME AT THE ZOO

*Saturday, 1:00 – 1:30 p.m.: CBS*
*Debut: 1/10/53; Cancellation: 5/30/53*
*Producer: Jack Dolph*
*Director: Glen Bernard*
*Host: Jack Whitaker*

Originating locally on station WCAU, this show was broadcast live from the Philadelphia Zoo. Freeman Shelly, the zoo director, took the show's host, Jack Whitaker, and three children on tours of different sections of the enclosure. Episodes focused on a specific animal or group of animals. Shelly described each species and its habits and answered questions posed by the children.

Whitaker remained with the CBS network as a sportscaster until recently, when he moved to ABC's sports department. Arnold Raybin was principal writer for the series.

## ROD BROWN, ROCKET RANGER

*Saturday, 11:30 – 12:00 noon: CBS*
*Debut: 4/10/53, Cancellation: 5/29/54*
*Executive Producer: William Dozier*
*Producer: George Beck*

*Cast*
Ranger Rod Brown . . . . . . .Cliff Robertson
Ranger Frank Boyle . . . . . .Bruce Hall
Commander Swift . . . . . . . .John Boruff
Ranger Wilbur Wormser
  ("Wormsy") . . . . . . . . . .Jack Weston
Just before 5:00 a.m. every Saturday morning, a small group of actors and technicians would file into a building on Manhattan's upper Fifth Avenue to rehearse this live, Kellogg-sponsored "cops-and-robbers" space series. Playing in one of his earliest television roles, Cliff Robertson received $150 per episode for impersonating Rod Brown. Operating from Omega Base, his team patrolled the galaxy to search out perpetrators of evil and bring them to justice. The team occasionally battled ferocious wild

*Rod Brown, Rocket Ranger*: Cliff Robertson as Rod Brown. (Courtesy of George Gould.)

animals on planets with unusual landscapes. Robertson has performed many major roles since then, including the title role in the film, *Charly,* and leads in the film *Three Days of The Condor* and the ABC-TV mini-series, *Washington: Behind Closed Doors.*

This series was filmed with a video-matting technique called Chroma-Key, a TV special effect that superimposes one picture over another. The technique placed the actors in scenes with miniature sets and models, enlarged electronically to the proper scale.

After the show's cancellation in 1954, William Dozier, then a senior programming executive at CBS, left the network to form Greenways Productions. His company went on to produce a number of satirical TV series, including *The Green Hornet.* Seeking an athletic Oriental to play the hero's houseboy Kato, Dozier discovered a young man giving karate demonstrations in Long Beach, New York. He signed him, little realizing that the fame of *Bruce Lee* would far outlive *The Green Hornet.* Supporting player Jack Weston ("Wormsey") went on to play roles in TV's *The Twilight Zone* and *79 Park Avenue,* and in the motion pictures *Wait Until Dark* and *The Four Seasons.* He has also appeared on Broadway in *The Ritz* and *The Floating Light Bulb.*

## THERE'S ONE IN EVERY FAMILY

*Saturday, 11:00 – 11:30 a.m.: CBS*
*Debut: 9/29/52; Cancellation: 6/12/53*
*Producer: Richard Levine*
*Host: John Reed King*

The exceptional abilities of family members was a source of humor and entertainment in this game show. Contestants demonstrated their unique verbal or theatrical talents to a studio audience, whose applause was registered on a meter to select the best competitor. He or she was then declared the "One in that Family." Finalists were pitted against each other in an elimination question-and-answer session to select a final winner, who was awarded a grand prize.

# 1953-1954 Season

*The Pinky Lee Show*: Pinky Lee. (Courtesy of Pinky Lee.)

## THE PINKY LEE SHOW

**Monday-Saturday,** *10:00 – 10:30 a.m.:*
  *NBC*
**Debut:** *1/4/54;* **Cancellation:** *5/11/56*
**Producers:** *Lee Wainer and Larry White*
**Host:** *Pinky Lee*
**Regulars:** *Roberts Shore, Mel Koonitz, Barbara Luke, Jimmy Brown, Jane Howard.*

Clown Pinky Lee, born Pincus Leff, was a natural comic entertainer who had made his name in vaudeville. Dressed in baggy pants, checkered coat and a matching tweed porkpie hat, he seemed to thoroughly enjoy working with a lively young audience.

His television career began with the 1950 prime-time offering *The Pinky Lee Show*. From 1951 to 1953 he co-hosted *Those Two*, a 15-minute musical variety series, with Vivian Blaine. It was here that he impressed Josh White, the young son of producer Larry White. White Senior decided to follow his son's suggestion to track Pinky down in New York. Soon after, the show made its debut. Produced in front of a live audience, it proved to be an ideal environment for Lee, who proceeded to involve cast, technicians and audience in his humorous routines, jokes and dance and comedy sketches.

His show contained a regular segment titled Mr. and Mrs. Grumpy. Mr. Grumpy owned everything: the local bank, the department store, even the circus where Pinky worked as a clown. Lee's dramatic powers were such that in one episode the studio audience and TV crew were reduced to tears. Mean Grumpy and friends drove off on vacation, leaving Pinky behind, who stood sadly at center stage holding a small suitcase.

Pinky became so popular that he was invited to be the featured guest on the **Gumby** show (1956/57). This series was produced on the opposite coast, which meant that Lee had to arrive in New York on Fridays for his Saturday morning appearances and immediately fly back to Los Angeles to continue work on his own program. He survived this rigorous routine for 13 weeks before collapsing in front of the cameras. After this, he began to slow down his schedule. The series was cancelled in 1956. Lee continued to host local Los Angeles shows throughout the 1960s.

*The Pinky Lee Show*: Pinky Lee and guest. (Courtesy of Pinky Lee.)

# ROCKY JONES, SPACE RANGER

*Saturday, 10:30–11:00 a.m.: NBC*
*Debut: 2/27/54; Cancellation: 4/17/54*
*Producer: Roland Reed*

## Cast

Rocky Jones . . . . . . . . . . . . .Richard Crane
Winky . . . . . . . . . . . . . . . .Scott Beckett
Vena Ray . . . . . . . . . . . . . .Sally Mansfield
Bobby . . . . . . . . . . . . . . . .Robert Lyden
Professor Newton . . . . . . . .Maurice Cass
Yarra . . . . . . . . . . . . . . . . .Dian Fauntelle
Other players: Crystal Reeves, Ralph Brooks, Robert S. Carson

Set in the 21st century, this science fantasy show revolved around Rocky Jones, Chief of the Space Rangers, a uniformed group of men and women recruited to police the solar system. Patrolling the galaxy in the "Orbit Jet," Rocky and his companions meted out impartial justice to lawbreakers and protection to law-abiding inhabitants of the system.

This filmed series was shot at the Hal Roach studios, where many of the Little Rascals and Laurel and Hardy films were made. The studio no longer exists. Prior to this venture, producer Roland Reed had specialized in commercials. Experienced in shooting economically and quickly, he brought the show in at a cost of approximately $8,000 per episode, a remarkable achievement considering the science fiction gimmickry required.

*Rocky Jones, Space Ranger*: Rocky Jones and Vena Ray. (Courtesy of Viacom International, Inc.)

## WINKY DINK AND YOU

*Saturday, 11:00–11:30 a.m.: CBS*
*Debut: 10/10/53; Cancellation: 4/27/57*
*Producers: Jack Barry, Dan Enright, Ed Friendly*
*Host: Jack Barry*
*Assistants: Mike McBean and Dayton Allen*

Television producers are always looking for new gimmicks to lock an audience into a particular show. One of the most ingenious "hooks" of all was the "Winky Dink Kit" which was also a profitable merchandising tie-in.

Winky Dink was an animated cartoon child, always accompanied by his dog, Woofer. Each episode found the young hero in trouble and requiring a vital object to effect his escape. Host Jack Barry would then ask viewers to take the clear plastic sheet from their kits and place it over the television screen. They then drew in the life-saving prop, using the crayon provided. When the show was over, the viewer erased the drawing from the plastic overlay, using the cloth thoughtfully included in the kit, purchased by mail order. To further involve the young audience, a word or series of letters suddenly would appear on the screen. Barry then instructed viewers to trace the letters onto the plastic sheet to receive a secret message. The live-action segment of the show featured comedy sketches performed by Jack Barry, with Dayton Allen as his incompetent assistant Mr. Bungle.

After the show was cancelled in 1957, a five-minute edition of the animated portion appeared in syndication until 1969. Barry and Dan Enright went on to form their own entertainment company, producing mainly game shows, including the highly successful *Tic Tac Dough, Twenty One,* and *Generation Gap.*

*Winky Dink and You:* A card advertising the return of Winky Dink in 1969. (Courtesy of Avalon Industries, Inc.)

# ANDY'S GANG

*Saturday, 9:30 – 10:00 a.m.: NBC*
*Debut: 8/20/55; Cancellation: 12/31/60*
*Producer/Director: Frank Ferrin*
*Host: Andy Devine*
**Voices**

Froggy, the Gremlin ......*Andy Devine*
Gunga Ram .............*Nino Marcell*
Rama .................*Vito Scotti*
The Maharajah .........*Lou Krugman*
The Poet...............*Alan Reed*
The Teacher............*Billy Gilbert*
Buster Brown ...........*Jerry Marin*
Tige ..................*Bud Tollefson*
Midnight ...............*June Foray*
Old Grandie ............*June Foray*

**Other voices:** *Joe Mazzuca, Peter Coo, Billy Race, Paul Cavanaugh*

Andy's Gang was a continuation of **Smilin' Ed's Gang** (1949/50), retitled after rotund Andy Devine replaced host Ed McConnell, who died in 1954. In its original format the program ran as *The Buster Brown TV Show with Smilin' Ed McConnell and the Buster Brown Gang*—hardly a succinct title. *Smilin' Ed's Gang* first aired in 1950 and ran on three of the networks in both prime time and Saturday mornings. It then returned to its original home at NBC.

Andy Devine had formerly been Wild Bill Hickock's companion, Jingles, in the syndicated TV series of that name. Frank Ferrin continued to produce and increased his directorial role in the program, which retained the sponsorship of Buster Brown Shoes.

Played in a clubhouse setting, the series consisted of comedy sketches, songs, stories and musical interludes. Added to this later NBC version of the show were storyteller Uncle Fishface and a loyal but usually unlucky mutt called Puddles.

---

*Andy's Gang: Andy Devine and Midnight, the cat. (Courtesy of Brown Group, Inc.)*

# CAPTAIN GALLANT OF THE FOREIGN LEGION

*Sunday, 5:00 – 5:30 p.m.: NBC*
*Debut: 2/13/55; Cancellation: 9/21/63*
*Producer: Harry Saltzman and Serge Glyson*

**Cast**
Captain Michael
  Gallant .............*Buster Crabbe*
Cuffy Sanders .........*Cullen Crabbe*
Private First Class,
  Fuzzy Knight ........*Fuzzy Knight*
Sergeant Du Val .......*Gilles Queant*
Carla ................*Norma Eberhardt*
The Colonel ...........*Roger Trevielle*

Buster Crabbe, known for his portrayals of *Flash Gordon, Buck Rogers, Tarzan* and *Billy, the Kid* played Captain Gallant, the bold and dashing commander of the North African headquarters of the French Foreign Legion. He was assisted by his ward Cuffy (played by Crabbe's real-life son Cullen), whose father was a Foreign Legion officer who had been killed in action.

This adventure series was unique in that it was shot on location, mostly in the Sahara desert, as well as in Spain and Italy. It resembled a traditional western, however, with the Legion (cowboys) pitted against the Arabs (Indians). Camels replaced horses, and djellabahs were *de rigueur*, rather than loin cloths and feathers.

65 half-hour episodes of the series were completed, with the sponsorship of H.J. Heinz. In syndication, the show became *Foreign Legionnaire.*

Crabbe Senior was a superb athlete—witness the range of movie roles he performed. His acting career began after winning gold medals in the swimming competition of the 1932 Olympics. Now residing in Arizona, he returned to the small screen to play the role of a pilot in the late 1970s TV version of *Buck Rogers.* Producer Harry Saltzman is best remembered for his partnership with Albert Broccoli in the production of nine James Bond movies, including *Goldfinger, From Russia with Love, Live and Let Die,* and *You Only Live Twice.*

*Captain Gallant and the Foreign Legion:* Capt. Michael Gallant and his ward, Cuffy Sanders. (Courtesy of Buster Crabbe.)

# CAPTAIN MIDNIGHT

*Saturday, 11:00 – 11:30 a.m.: CBS*
*Debut: 9/4/54; Cancellation: 5/12/56*
*Producers: George Billson and Screen Gems*

**Cast**

| | |
|---|---|
| Captain Midnight | . . . . . . . . Richard Webb |
| Ichabod ("Icky") Mudd | . . . . Sid Melton |
| Tut | . . . . . . . . . . . . . . . . . . . . Olan Soule |
| Chuck Ramsey | . . . . . . . . . . Renee Beard |
| Marcia Stanhope | . . . . . . . . Jan Shepard |

CAPTAIN MIDNIGHT (RICHARD WEBB)
TELEVISION - 1952-1957

*Captain Midnight*: Richard Webb in the title role. (Courtesy of Ovaltine Products Corp.)

"Justice through Strength and Courage" was the motto of this cold-war era science fiction series. Captain Midnight was the embodiment of the American way. Screen Gems, the TV arm of Columbia Pictures, had originally conceived of a younger hero. But Richard Webb, a real World War II flying ace, had the looks and real-life experience to bring off the role, and he was instrumental in the program's great success.

As leader of the Secret Squadron, Midnight combed the globe piloting his "Silver Dart" aircraft, flushing out spies, rescuing captured nuclear scientists, and vanquishing secret enemy agents. Viewers were encouraged to join the Squadron, which entitled them to receive a secret coded message at the close of each episode. Using a decoder (supplied for 25 cents and the seal from a jar of Ovaltine, the program's sponsor), Squadron members could learn what was in store for them the following week.

Captain Midnight began life on radio as Captain Albright, a mythical World War I pilot. Originating in Chicago over the Mutual Broadcasting System (and also sponsored by Ovaltine), the program aired in 1938. Ed Prentiss was the first to play the intrepid hero, and Paul Barnes was the last, before the radio series went off the air.

On network television the series ran on both ABC and CBS. It premiered on Saturday morning and later found a receptive adult audience in prime time. Because Ovaltine had copyrighted the Captain Midnight name, the syndicated reruns aired as *Jet*

*Jackson, Flying Commando.* Screen Gems went to considerable lengths to dub out the words "Captain Midnight." Apparently the only prints still in existence are those identified as "Jet Jackson."

Richard Webb went on to write books, including an autobiography. He also played roles in TV's *Border Patrol* and in the theatrical movie *Beware The Blob,* directed by Larry Hagman (J. R. Ewing of *Dallas*).

## CHILDREN'S CORNER

*Saturday, 10:30–11:00 a.m.: NBC*
*Debut: 8/20/55; Cancellation: 4/28/56*
**Conception/Producers:** *Fred Rogers and Josie Carey*
**Hostess:** *Josie Carey*
**Voices/Puppeteers:** *Fred Rogers and Josie Carey*

*Children's Corner* was conceived as a cozy and reassuring environment in a teeming, jumbled world. It was inhabited by animals, all of whom were glove puppets, and one or two adults.

Ms. Carey hosted the series, with Rogers hidden from the camera operating the puppets. When Rogers appeared on-camera, he was always in costume.

The pair collaborated on scripts and music that encouraged in children a simple sense of morality and decency. The program also introduced children to foreign languages and other cultures. The docile Daniel S. Tiger, Grandpere the skunk, and Rogers and Carey eschewed stereotypes and encouraged young viewers to assess for themselves the merits of an individual or situation.

*Children's Corner* was originally created for Pittsburgh's WQED, now a prominent Public Television station. It first aired on WQED on April 1, 1954 and ran on that station until 1961. In 1955 NBC was looking for a summer replacement for their successful *Jerry Mahoney's Club House/Winchell and Mahoney,* and the network engaged Rogers and Carey to produce another *Children's Corner.* Also aired on Saturdays, the new program became so popular that the network decided to hold it over. The innova-

tive writing team was soon commuting between Pittsburgh and New York, creating two separate editions of similar material. In 1955 the original program won the Sylvania Award as the best locally produced children's show in the country. The show ran

*Children's Corner*: Fred Rogers, Josie Carey and Daniel S. Tiger. (Courtesy of Fred Rogers.)

Fred Rogers on the set of his popular PBS show, *Mister Rogers' Neighborhood.*

for seven years on PBS and was the blueprint for the even more successful *Mr. Rogers Neighborhood,* which began life on CBC in Canada.

Rogers subsequently became an influential voice in educational television, producing many PBS specials for children and adults. For his contribution to educational children's television programming, he won an Emmy in 1980. In addition to his television work, Rogers is a minister of the United Presbyterian Church, ordained in 1963. He contemplates a ministry directed specifically to children and the family unit by way of the mass media. As of 1983, more than 250 PBS stations carried *Mr. Rogers' Neighborhood.* The show is funded by such corporate organs as the Sears-Roebuck Foundation, and Johnson and Johnson.

# COMMANDO CODY—SKY MARSHALL OF THE UNIVERSE

*Saturday, 11:00 – 11:30 a.m.: NBC*
*Debut: 7/16/55; Cancellation: 10/8/55*
*Producer: Franklin Andreon*

## Cast

| | |
|---|---|
| Commando Cody/Jeff King | Judd Holdren |
| Joan Albright | Aline Towne |
| Ted Richards | William Schallert |
| Retik, Ruler of the Moon | Gregory Grey |
| Dr. Varney | Peter Brocco |
| Henderson | Craig Kelly |

Both natural and man-made catastrophes were the fearless Cody's territory. The single-minded sky marshall patrolled the universe and frequently came face-to-face with Retik, the evil Ruler of the moon.

This series was produced by Republic Pictures, owners of a library of theatrical science fiction footage, to inexpensively capitalize on the success of such mid-1950s TV shows as ***Captain Midnight*** (1954/55) and *Rocky Jones*. The writers of the series incorporated many gadgets to assist Cody in his duties, including an ever-present mask to hide his secret identity. He also wore an elaborate dial on his tunic, which controlled ascent and descent, and a rocket back-pack. The program's dated theatrical car chases and alien encounters did not endear it to TV audiences.

Holdren had previously played the lead in Columbia Pictures' theatrical version of *Captain Video* (1951). William Schallert later became a frequent sight on the *Patty Duke Show* and *The Nancy Drew Mysteries*. He was President of the Screen Actors Guild from 1979 to 1981.

*Commando Cody, Sky Marshall of the Universe*: Judd Holdren as Commando Cody and Aline Towne as Joan Albright. (Courtesy of National Telefilm Associates.)

# JERRY MAHONEY'S CLUB HOUSE

*Saturday, 10:00–10:30 a.m.: NBC*
*Debut: 11/20/54; Cancellation: 2/25/56*
*Producer: Paul Winchell*
*Host: Paul Winchell*

Maintaining the basic format of his previous shows, Paul Winchell returned to the Saturday morning line-up with this series. He had spent the preceding four years with NBC as the star of *The Paul Winchell and Jerry Mahoney Spiedel Show* and a subsequent game show. Both gave equal billing to his wooden companion. Here the setting was a small Midwestern social club, with puppet Mahoney as president and his friend Knucklehead Smith shouldering the responsibilities as Vice President. Each week the club entertained a different neighbor, played by Winchell, who dropped by to shoot the breeze. Winchell would vary his costume according to the occupation and financial circumstances of his characters.

The show ran for two seasons in this format. Repackaged, it moved to ABC as *The Paul Winchell Show* (1957/58).

# THE SOUPY SALES SHOW

*Monday-Friday, 7:00–7:15 p.m.: ABC*
*Producers: Alan Bregman, Soupy Sales*
*Debut: 7/4/55; Cancellation: 8/26/55*
*Return: 10/3/59; Cancellation: 4/1/61*
*Return: 1/62; Cancellation: 4/13/62*
*Host: Soupy Sales*
*Assistant: Clyde Adler*

Entertainer Soupy Sales had originally planned to be a journalist, but he proved to be a born stand-up comedian whose inspired silliness delighted a generation of young viewers. His uniform for this program included an oversize polka-dot bow tie and a flattened top hat. What made him famous, however, was an endless supply of cream pies that graced some of the most famous faces in show business.

After TV appearances in Cincinnati, Sales debuted with his own show in Detroit and went network as a summer replacement for the highly successful **Kukla, Fran and Ollie** (1948/49). The show went out live and featured a number of puppet characters, including White Fang and Black Tooth, two dogs with opposing temperaments; Marilyn Monwolf; Herman, the Flea; Willie, the Worm; Pookie, the Lion, and Hippy, the Hippo.

Sales had hosted a number of shows over the years, both network and syndicated, in various formats. In 1950 he hosted *Soupy's Soda Shop*, a teenage dance program, followed by *Club Nothing*, a 45-minute talk show spiced with his zany humor and antics.

Since the show's cancellation, Sales has been active in game shows, as both a host and a panelist. In the 1960s, he created a popular dance called "The Mouse."

# UNCLE JOHNNY COONS

*Saturday, 10:00–10:30 a.m.: CBS*
*Debut: 9/4/54; Cancellation: 12/3/55 (CBS)*
*Return: 3/3/56; Cancellation: 12/1/56 (NBC)*
*Producer: James Green and CNC Productions*
*Host: Johnny Coons*
*Voices: Johnny Coons*
*Announcer: Bruce Roberts*

This Chicago-based live series featured ventriloquist Johnny Coons as host and puppet operator. Each episode featured stories, silent films, cartoons and dramatic interludes, designed to teach youngsters moral responsibility. Between sketches and film inserts, Coons played comedy routines with George Dummy, his wooden "partner," Blackie, George's invisible dog, and Joe, the "unseen giant."

Coons' relaxed brand of comedy was a vehicle which brought to his young audience

*The Soupy Sales Show*: Soupy Sales and friend. (Courtesy of Soupy Sales.)

thoughts of a deeper significance. The show was an outgrowth of the local *Noontime Comics,* a program aimed at a lunchtime family audience. Restaurants and sandwich shops often left the set on during this show, testifying to its popularity. Originally titled *Life with Uncle Johnny Coons,* the series debuted on the CBS Saturday schedule in 1954. The first two words of the title were dropped shortly thereafter. Coons provided the voices for every character, Ray Chan wrote the scripts and Bill Newton handled the visuals. Coons, Chan and Newton joined forces in 1950 to form their own production company. Called CNC, it produced similar shows until the company disbanded in April 1959.

Coons also starred in *Uncle Mistletoe and His Adventures,* which ran on ABC in 1950. In addition, he has appeared in commercials for such companies as Lever Brothers, sponsors of the *Uncle Johnny Coons Show.* He died in July 1975.

*Uncle Johnny Coons:* Johnny Coons and George Dummy with a young audience. (Courtesy of Ray Chan.)

*Uncle Johnny Coons:* Coons going for a ride. (Courtesy Ray Chan.)

1955-1956 Season

# THE ADVENTURES OF ROBIN HOOD

*Saturday, 11:30–12:00 noon: CBS*
*Debut: 9/26/55; Cancellation: 9/22/58*
*Producer: Sidney Cole, Hannah Weinstein*

*Cast*
Robin Hood . . . . . . . .*Richard Greene*
Friar Tuck . . . . . . . . .*Alexander Gauge*
Little John . . . . . . . . .*Archie Duncan*
Maid Marion
    Fitzwater . . . . . . . .*Bernadette O'Farrell*
                           *Patricia Driscoll*
Prince John . . . . . . . .*Donald Pleasance*
                           *Hubert Gregg*
The Sheriff
    of Nottingham   . . . .*Alan Wheatley*
Sir Richard The
    Lion-Hearted  . . . . .*Ian Hunter*
Lady Genevieve . . . . .*Gillian Sterrett*
Will Scarlet  . . . . . . . .*Paul Eddington*
King Arthur . . . . . . . .*Peter Asher*
Duncan,
    the Scotsman  . . . . .*Hugh McDermott*

This television series was based on the classic English folk tale by Roger Lancelyn Green. Set in Britain in 1191, it told the story of how Robin Hood used Sherwood Forest as the base of his operations, and how he organized a small band of free-born Englishmen to battle the villainy of Prince John.

The conflict began after King Richard the Lion-Hearted entrusted his kingdom to his ally Longchamps, when he went off to the Holy Land to fight in the Crusades. This angered Richard's brother John, who had expected the lands to be entrusted to him. While Richard passed through Austria, he was taken prisoner by John's villainous confidant Sir Leopold and held captive in Vienna. With Richard safely in custody, John took control of the kingdom and began to alienate the Saxons with punitive and illegal taxes. Citizens not complying with Prince John's demands suffered tragic consequences. Sir Robin of Locksley was appalled by this gross exploitation. When he opposed the Prince, the tyrant promptly declared him an outlaw. To avoid arrest or harrassment, Sir Robin went about in a cape to shield his identity. Hence the name "Robin Hood."

Retreating to Gallows Oak in Sherwood Forest, Robin recruited his band of Merry Men, who swore allegiance to Richard. They then began the task of raising money to organize a force to rescue their captive King, restore him to the throne and rid them of the tyrant. The money, of course, came from the tyrant's notorious tax collectors, especially the Sheriff of Nottingham.

Filmed in England with a British cast, the series employed researchers to ensure period authenticity. The designs of costumes, swords, daggers and other props used were drawn from illustrations and literature of the period. *The Adventures of Robin Hood* was originally a success on CBS's prime-time schedule. Its dramatic action, swordsmanship and fast-moving action ensured its popularity on the Saturday schedule. The show was subsequently syndicated under the title *Sherwood Forest*.

Producer Hannah Weinstein later moved on to feature films. She co-produced Columbia Pictures' 1980 box-office success *Stir Crazy,* starring Richard Pryor and Gene Wilder.

# CAPTAIN KANGAROO

*Monday-Friday, 8:00–9:00 p.m.: CBS*
*Debut: 10/3/55; Still Running*
*Supplier: Robert Keeshan Associates*
*Producers: Jack Miller, Jon Stone, Bob*
    *Claver, Dave Connell, Sam Gibbon, Al*
    *Hyslop, Jim Hirschfield*

*Cast*
Captain
    Kangaroo. . . .*Bob Keeshan*
Mr. Green
    Jeans . . . . . . .*Hugh "Lumpy" Brannum*
Debbie . . . . . . . .*Debbie Weems*
Dennis . . . . . . . .*Cosmo Allegretti*

*Captain Kangaroo*: Robert Keeshan in the title role. (Courtesy of Robert Keeshan Associates.)

*Captain Kangaroo*: An early photo of the Captain. (Courtesy of Robert Keeshan Associates.)

*Mr. Baxter.....James E. Wall*

**Puppets:** *Mr. Moose, Bunny Rabbit, Miss Worm, Miss Frog*

In the annals of children's television, 1955 is a landmark year. It marks the debut of what has become the longest running children's program in television history.

Bob Keeshan plays the gentle, warmhearted Captain wearing his trademark jacket, whose large pockets are full of unexpected goodies. The series, always low-key, stresses gentleness, with the emphasis on entertainment and education. The show has changed little over the years, and it still offers charades, sketches, puppets and cartoons. Guest stars have included Alan Arkin, Carol Channing, Marlo Thomas, Imogene Coca, Doug Henning, Eli Wallach and Pearl Bailey.

Mr. Green Jeans has been with the series since the beginning. He introduces animals, while portraying a good-natured and innovative farmer who loves to invent things. Cosmo Allegretti portrays the bumbling apprentice, who is everyone's unwitting thorn-in-the-side. As chief puppeteer, Allegretti is also responsible for the voices and manipulation of such other characters as Bunny Rabbit, Mr. Moose, Miss Frog, Mr. Whispers and Word Bird. Cartoon segments include *Mighty Manfred, the Wonder Dog;* and Terrytoons' famous creation, *Tom Terrific.*

Prior to Captain Kangaroo, Keeshan had played Clarabell on the hit children's show **Howdy Doody** (1947/48). He also

hosted two local New York shows, *Time For Fun* and *Tinker's Workshop.* During the 1964/1965 season he played the lead in another children's show, **Mister Mayor.**

In the fall of 1981, against much opposition from parents, educators and children, CBS shortened and rescheduled *Captain Kangaroo* to an earlier slot. This award-winning show was retitled *Wake Up the Captain.* Sadly, the move reflects a reduced commitment to even the most tried and successful innovative children's programming.

## CHOOSE UP SIDES

*Saturday, 12:00 – 12:30 p.m.: NBC*
*Debut: 1/7/56; Cancellation: 3/31/56*
*Producers: Bill Todman; Mark Goodson*
*Host: Gene Rayburn*

This children's game show presented two competing teams, the Space Pilots and the Bronco Busters (originally called the Cowboys and the Space Rangers). The winning team received prizes for successfully completing various stunts and tasks. The show was a children's version of *Beat The Clock,* an adult game show also produced by Goodson-Todman.

*Choose Up Sides* originally ran as a local show over New York's WCBS, with Dean Miller as host. When the show moved to NBC, Gene Rayburn became the emcee, while continuing as announcer on Steve Allen's *Tonight Show.* Rayburn later became master of ceremonies for the *Match Game.* He has also hosted both the *Miss Universe* and *Miss World* pageants.

Bill Todman (who died in 1980) and Mark Goodson were responsible for some of the most successful game shows in television history. From the Goodson-Todman stable came such series as *What's My Line?* (1950– 67), *To Tell the Truth* (1956– 67), *The Price is Right* (1956– 64), *Family Feud* (1976– ) and many others.

*Choose Up Sides*: Gene Rayburn, circa 1956. (Courtesy of Gene Rayburn.)

*Fury*: Bobby Diamond and Fury. (Photo courtesy of ITC Entertainment.)

# FURY

**Saturday,** 11:30 – 12:00 noon: NBC
**Debut:** 10/15/55; **Cancellation:** 9/3/66
**Executive Producer:** Leon Fromkess
**Producer:** Irving Cummings
**Supplier:** Edward Small and Television Programs of America

*Cast*

| | |
|---|---|
| Jim Newton | Peter Graves |
| Joey Newton | Bobby Diamond |
| Pete | William Fawcett |
| Helen Watkins | Ann Robinson |
| Pee Wee | Jimmy Baird |
| Packey Lambert | Roger Mobley |
| Harriet Newton | Nan Leslie |
| The Sheriff | James Seay |
| Deputy Sheriff | Guy Teague |
| Fury, the horse | Beauty |

While playing baseball, a group of boys accidentally break a window. Fearing punishment, they put the blame on Joey, an innocent orphan who is wrongly suspected of being a troublemaker. Rancher Jim Newton witnesses the accident and intercedes on the boy's behalf, clearing his name. He learns that Joey is an orphan, and compassionately returns home with the boy to Broken Wheel Ranch. He eventually adopts Joey and gives him a beautiful black stallion, with which he hopes to win the boy's trust and teach him a sense of responsibility. Joey and the horse, Fury, become inseparable. (The stallion, named Beauty, was owned by trainer Ralph McCutcheon. He played Black Beauty in the big screen version and lived to be 29 years old.) Episodes followed Joey's personal growth and the adventures and new experiences he and Fury embarked upon.

This television favorite entertained millions every Saturday morning. It is still syndicated all over the world, often under the title *Brave Stallion*.

The success in recent years of the films *The Black Stallion* and *Black Stallion II* confirm the never-ending appeal of this classic story. *Fury* was one of the earliest series to offer realistic role models for children to emulate. Creator/Producer Irving Cummings Jr. never lectured his audience, but in each of the 114 episodes he stressed the importance of such moral values as responsibility, thoughtfulness and sportsmanship, as well as the virtues of good horsemanship. Cummings later created another children's show about a horse called *Thunder,* which was broadcast in the late 1970s on NBC's Saturday morning schedule.

Bobby Diamond (Joey) gave up television for the law. Roger Mobley (Packey) has worked primarily for the Disney organization, with roles in *Emil and The Detectives, The Treasure of the San Bosco Reef* and *The Kids Who Knew Too Much.* Peter Graves, brother of James Arness, (star of TV's classic Western, *Gunsmoke*) starred in CBS's *Mission: Impossible.* He has also appeared in various TV movies, pilots and commercials.

# THE MICKEY MOUSE CLUB

**Monday – Friday,** 5:00 – 6:00 p.m.: ABC
**Debut:** 10/3/55; **Cancellation:** 9/24/59
**Executive Producer:** Walt Disney
**Producers:** Bill Walsh, Dick Darley
**Supplier:** Walt Disney Productions
**Host:** Jimmie Dodd
**Co-Host:** Roy Williams (The Big Mouseketeer)
**Assistant:** Bob Amsberry

*The Mouseketeers:* Annette Funicello, Darlene Gillespie, Carl "Cubby" O'Brien, Karen Pendleton, Bobby Burgess, Tommy Cole, Cheryl Holdridge, Lynn Ready, Doreen Tracy, Linda Hughes, Lonnie Burr, Bonnie Lynn Fields, Sharon Baird, Ronnie Young, Jay Jay Solari, Margene Storey, Nancy Abbate, Billie Jean Beanblossom, Mary Espinosa, Bonnie Lou Kern, Mary Lou Sartori, Bronson Scott, Dennis Day, Dickie Dodd, Michael Smith, Ronald Steiner, Mark Sutherland, Don Underhill, Sherry Allen, Paul Peterson, *Judy Harriett, John Lee Johnson, Eileen Diamond, Charley Laney, Larry Larsen, Don Agrati (Don Grady).*

**Voice of Jiminy Cricket:** *Cliff Edwards*
**Voice of Mickey Mouse:** *Jim MacDonald*
**Narrator of Mickey Mouse Newsreel:** *Hal Gibney*
**Special News Correspondent:** *Dick Metzzi*

Walt Disney's famous cartoon character Mickey Mouse, an international favorite since the 1920s, was the star of this television series. The show consisted of music, songs, cartoons, children's news features, adventure serials and appearances by guest celebrities. The supporting cast of Mouseketeers provided jobs and acting entrees for a large ensemble of young performers. The series was telecast in both 60 and 30 minute formats and was seen in various time periods on the ABC network during its four year run, including Saturday mornings.

After the series ended in 1959, it resurfaced in syndication in 1962 and ran in local markets until 1965. It was again revived in syndication in 1975. The following year a syndicated spin-off was produced, entitled *The New Mickey Mouse Club.* The new version introduced 12 new Mouseketeers— including minority members—and aired first-run Disney cartoons and films.

The original *Mickey Mouse Club* regularly featured serials. These included *Adventures in Dairyland, The Adventures of Clint and Mac, Annette, Border Collie, The Boys of the Western Sea, Corky and White Shadow, The Hardy Boys and The Mystery of Ghost Farm, Moochie of the Little League, Moochie of Pop Warner Football, The Secret of Mystery Lake, Spin and Marty* and *What I Want to Be.*

# THE MIGHTY MOUSE PLAYHOUSE

**Saturday, 10:00 – 10:30 a.m.: CBS**
**Debut: 12/10/55; Cancellation: 9/2/67**
**Supplier:** *Bill Weiss and Terrytoons*
**Voice of Mighty Mouse:** *Tom Morrison*

In the wake of live-action superheroes came this appealing super-rodent, whose powers included singing operas. Battling enemies

and saving his friends from harm, while singing all the while, were stock-in-trade for Mighty Mouse. Over the years, many talented animators contributed to this Terrytoons series, including Ralph Bakshi, who later made several full-length adult cartoon movies, including *Fritz the Cat* (1972), *Heavy Traffic* (1973), *Lord of The Rings* (1978), and *American Pop* (1981).

Toward the end of its lengthy network run, the show was renamed *Mighty Heroes*. Although it was severely castigated in 1959 by *The National Parent-Teacher* magazine, UNICEF saw fit to honor Mighty Mouse as its official ambassador in 1961 and 1962.

In 1979, Filmation produced an updated version titled *The New Adventures of Mighty Mouse and Heckle and Jeckle*. The two crows (Heckle and Jeckle) had also originated with Terrytoons. On the demise of that studio they too were acquired by Filmation. In this reworking of the rodent's exploits, Mighty Mouse was denied his operatic outbursts.

*Mighty Mouse Playhouse*: Mighty Mouse. (Courtesy of Viacom International, Inc.)

## MY FRIEND FLICKA

**Saturday,** *1:00 – 1:30 p.m.: CBS*
**Debut:** *2/10/56;* **Cancellation:** *2/8/57*
  *(CBS)*
**Return:** *9/22/57;* **Cancellation:** *5/18/58*
  *(NBC)*
**Producers:** *Alan A. Armor, Peter Packer,*
  *Sam White and Herman Schlom*
**Supplier:** *20th Century-Fox*

*Cast*
Rob McLaughlin . . . . . . Gene Evans
Nell McLaughlin . . . . . . Anita Louise
Ken McLaughlin . . . . . . Johnny Washbrook
Gus Broeberg . . . . . . . . Frank Ferguson
Hildy Broeberg . . . . . . . Pamela Beaird
Sheriff Walt Downey . . Hugh Sanders,
                                        Sidney Mason
U.S. Marshall . . . . . . . . Craig Duncan
Sgt. Tim O'Gara . . . . . Tudor Owen
Flicka, the horse . . . . . . Wahama

Set in Montana, this series was based on the popular Mary O'Hara stories, which had been made into a motion picture by Twentieth Century-Fox in 1943.

Episodes focussed on the growing relationship between young Ken McLaughlin and the horse given to him by his father. The gift was intended to teach the boy responsibility. The McLaughlin family lived on the Goose Bar Ranch. Episodes recounted the adventures of Ken and Flicka (which means "little girl" in Swedish). Conflicts in the lives of the McLaughlin family were explored and soap opera elements often intruded upon the adventure and action.

Although filmed in color, this series was aired in black and white while on prime time. This was due to lack of available color outlets on the CBS network. When the program moved to NBC's Saturday schedule, it was broadcast in color.

## TALES OF THE TEXAS RANGERS

*Saturday, 11:30 – 12:00 noon: CBS*
*Thursday, 5:00 – 5:30 p.m.: ABC*
*Monday, 7:30 – 8:00 p.m.: ABC*
*Debut: 9/3/55; Cancellation: 5/25/58*
  *(CBS)*
*Return: 10/58: Cancellation: 5/25/59*
  *(ABC)*
*Producers: Harry Ackerman, Jonal Seinfield, Colbert Clark*
*Supplier: Screen Gems*

*Cast*
*Ranger Jace Pearson* . . . . . . *Willard Parker*
*Ranger Clay Morgan* . . . . . . *Harry Lauter*

This western series was different than most in that its stories were drawn from the files of the Texas Rangers, the oldest law enforcement organization in North America. Its two rangers spanned 120 years of crime-fighting in the Old and New West—from the 1830s to the 1950s. The rangers were at home on horses galloping through mesa landscapes or in cars speeding at 90 mph on modern highways.

The program began as a radio serial in the early 1950s, with Joel McCrea as Ranger Pearson.

*My Friend Flicka* (left to right): Johnny Washbrook, Flicka, Anita Louise and Gene Evans. (Courtesy of DePatie-Freleng Enterprises, Inc.)

1956-1957 Season

# AMERICAN BANDSTAND

*Saturday, 12:30 – 1:30 p.m.: ABC*
*Debut: 8/5/57; Still running*
*Supplier: Dick Clark Productions*
*Host: Dick Clark*
*Announcers: Dick Clark and Charlie O'Donnell*

This landmark series is not only one of television's longest running programs, it is the first network show devoted exclusively to contemporary popular music. Most major music personalities have at one time or another appeared on American Bandstand, and it has made host Dick Clark a household name.

*American Bandstand* began in 1952 as a local show, on Philadelphia's ABC affiliate, WFIL. The original hosts, Bob Horn and Lee Stewart, were replaced in 1956 by Clark, who had been a disc jockey for a Philadelphia radio station. Clark's personality brought the show to prime-time network, where it remained for 13 weeks in 1957. It ran in the weekday schedule until September of 1963, when it moved to a Saturday morning slot. Primarily a showcase for rising popular musical groups and soloists, the program usually features one established act per show. It boasts a highly active participating audience as well.

*American Bandstand*: Dick Clark, the inspiration behind this successful show. (Courtesy of Dick Clark Productions.)

# CBS CARTOON THEATER

*Wednesday, 7:30–8:00 p.m.: CBS*
*Debut: 6/13/56; Cancellation: 9/5/56*
*Supplier: Terrytoons and CBS-TV*
*Host: Dick Van Dyke*
*Voices: Dayton Allen, Paul Frees*

This summer replacement, which had only a three-month network run, was television's first prime-time cartoon series.

Comedian Dick Van Dyke provided the linking passages, introducing characters from the Terrytoons Studio. These included *Heckle and Jeckle*, who were eventually given a series of their own. Others shown were *Gandy Goose, Sour Puss, Dinky Duck* and *Little Roquefort*. The program was the result of Terrytoons' sale to TV of its library of famous movie cartoons.

# CIRCUS BOY

*Sunday, 7:30–8:00 p.m.: NBC*
*Thursday, 7:30–8:00 p.m.: ABC*
*Saturday, 11:30–12:00 noon: NBC*
*Debut: 9/23/56; Cancellation: 9/8/57 (NBC)*
*Return: 9/19/57; Cancellation: 9/11/58 (ABC)*
*Return: 1958; Cancellation: 9/60 (NBC)*
*Producers: Herbert B. Leonard, Norman Blackburn*
*Supplier: Screen Gems*

*Cast*
Big Tim Champion . . . . .Robert Lowery
Joey, the clown . . . . . . . .Noah Beery, Jr.
Corky . . . . . . . . . . . . . . .Mickey Braddock
Pete . . . . . . . . . . . . . . . . .Guin "Big Boy" Williams
Circus Jack . . . . . . . . . . . .Andy Clyde

Corky, a 12-year old orphan, was the main attraction of this live show, set in a circus at the turn of the century. The young hero had been adopted by members of Big Tim Champion's traveling circus, after the death

of his parents in a high-wire accident. Big Tim became Corky's guardian and took a special interest in the boy.

Circus life was the background of this series, with Big Tim's band of animals and players moving from town to town. Although fictional, the program attempted to accurately show children what a busy, thriving circus was like. Corky developed a strong attachment to the baby elephant Bimbo, for whom he was water boy. Mickey Braddock, the young actor who played Corky, is better known as Mickey Dolenz, the diminutive singer and instrumentalist of the successful TV series *The Monkees* (1966–68).

*Circus Boy* began as an NBC prime-time series, then switched to ABC prime time. The program returned to NBC in 1958 as a Saturday morning series. Forty-nine episodes of *Circus Boy* were made, all in black and white, at a cost of $33,000 per show. It was filmed in Los Angeles and sponsored by Mars, the candy manufacturer.

Producer Herbert Leonard has a number of television series to his credit, including *Naked City, Route 66, The Adventures of Rin Tin Tin*, and, more recently, the television version of *Breaking Away*.

# CIRCUS TIME

*Thursday, 8:00–9:00 p.m.: ABC*
*Debut: 10/4/56; Cancellation: 6/27/57*
*Producer: Martin Stone*
*Host: Paul Winchell*

Ventriloquist and children's entertainer Paul Winchell hosted this prime-time variety series, accompanied by his inimitable wooden accomplices Jerry Mahoney and Knucklehead Smith. The series, set against the background of a circus, was an extravaganza of tigers. lions, circus performers and guest stars. Popular music played an important role in the show.

# THE GALEN DRAKE SHOW

*Saturday,* 7:00 – 7:30 *p.m.: ABC*
*Debut: 1/12/57; Cancellation: 5/11/57*
*Producer: Don Apel*

*Cast*
Host . . . . . . . . . . . . . *Galen Drake*
Soloists . . . . . . . . . *Stuart Foster, Rita Ellis*
Band . . . . . . . . . . . *The 3 Beaus and*
                          *a Peep*

Galen Drake, the great storyteller of radio, moved to television as the host of this children's variety series. The soloists and their accompanying band provided musical interludes. Drake also conducted interviews with such guests as Melvin Purvis, the famous F.B.I. G-Man, band-leader Paul Whiteman, and puppeteer Bil Baird, the man responsible for *Life with Snarky Parker* and *The Whistling Wizard.*

Drake wrote his own material, which encouraged children to reach beyond their experience and to develop adult interests. A great believer in the importance of the written word, Drake frequently mentioned things he'd learned from books. Perhaps he saw the inherent dangers that television posed for impressionable children.

The program started life on CBS radio in New York. The TV show was broadcast live from New York in front of an audience. Best Foods was the sponsor.

*The Galen Drake Show:* Galen Drake (center) and friends. (Courtesy Galen Drake.)

"THE NEW GERALD MCBOI
Pirates
Music
Comedy
U P A 'S
FIRST ANIMATED VARIE

BOING© SHOW"

c

INVENTORS

Circus

ART

Animals

SHOW

## THE GERALD MCBOING-BOING SHOW

*Sunday, 5:30–6:00 p.m.: CBS*
*Debut: 12/16/56; Cancellation: 10/3/58*
*Supplier: UPA Pictures*
*Voices: Marvin Miller*

Gerald McBoing-Boing originated in a story by Doctor Seuss, author of such children's classics as *The Cat in the Hat, Green Eggs and Ham* and *The Grinch Who Stole Christmas.*

McBoing-Boing, a curly-haired little boy, was introduced to the public in 1950, in a movie cartoon that won an Academy Award. United Productions of America (UPA) subsequently produced a series of theatrical films featuring the character. These were distributed by Columbia Pictures.

Gerald McBoing-Boing was a completely original animated cartoon character: instead of talking, he voiced sound effects, most of which sounded like "boing, boing!" After the success of his animated theatrical shorts, McBoing-Boing moved to the small screen. His TV series was comprised of UPA theatrical material and freshly conceived scripts.

In addition to McBoing, who served as host, the show included the animated adventures of The Twirlinger Twins and Dusty of the Circus. Educational segments included *Meet the Artist, Meet the Inventor,* and *Legends of Americans in the World.* These added instructional value to the entertainment. Much was made of the musical elements; most of the songs and instrumental pieces were composed especially for the show.

Stephen Bosustow, John Hubley, Ed Gershman and Art Babbit founded UPA in the 1940s. The studio was famous for the irascible *Mr. Magoo.* It also produced *Dick Tracy,* an animated cartoon version of Chester Gould's comic strip crime-fighter, which was syndicated in the early 1960s.

*Gerald McBoing-Boing*: Gerald McBoing-Boing. (Courtesy of UPA Pictures, Inc. [1982].)

# SUSAN'S SHOW

*Saturday, 11:00–11:30 a.m.: CBS*
*Debut: 5/4/57; Cancellation: 1/18/58*
*Producers: Paul Frumkin, Frank Atlass*
*Hostess: Susan Heinkel*

Susan Heinkel was the 12-year-old hostess of this fantasy series, comprised of songs, stories and *Popeye* cartoons. She was accompanied by her pet terrier Rusty and a friendly talking table, called Mr. Pegasis.

In each episode Susan and Rusty took a trip on her magic flying chair. At the mention of a magic word, the chair would transport them to Wonderville, a land containing a machine that showed cartoons and had an orchestra composed entirely of animal musicians.

The series originated locally on Chicago's station WBBM—a CBS affiliate—where it ran daily as *Susie's Show*. In this format Ms. Heinkel and the show won a number of Emmy awards. She was the youngest recipient of such an accolade. Going network, the show changed little except to move to a Saturday morning slot. Susan Heinkel is now married and lives in St. Louis.

*Susan's Show*: Susan Heinkel with characters from "Wonderville." (Courtesy of Paul Frumkin.)

1957 - 1958 Season

# GUMBY

**Saturday, 10:30 – 11:00 a.m.: NBC**
**Debut: 3/23/57; Cancellation: 11/16/57**
**Producer:** Art Clokey
**Hosts:** Bob Nicholson as Scotty McKee,
  Pinky Lee

This cute little green clay figure was introduced to television audiences on **Howdy
Doody** (1947/48), where he had his own
five-minute slot. The unusual character,
animated by stop-motion photography,
quickly built a popular following, sufficient to
launch him in his own show.

Bob Nicholson defected from *Howdy
Doody* to become host Scotty McKee. Each
episode was set in McKee's Fun Shop,
where his "master-pet" relationship with
Gumby was explored in a series of adventures. Gumby's pet was his beloved horse
Pokey, also a manipulated clay figure. Although not seen on network television for
some time, the character was kept alive by
producer Art Clokey during visits to colleges
and town community centers. Gumby's adventures were scheduled to be released to
the home video market in 1983 by Family
Home Entertainment. F.H.E's purchase of
the complete library includes the 1955 clay
animation classic *Gumbaysia*, which will also
be re-released.

Clokey was also the creator of *Davy and
Goliath,* one of the greatest successes in
syndicated children's broadcasting. *Davy
and Goliath* is still running today.

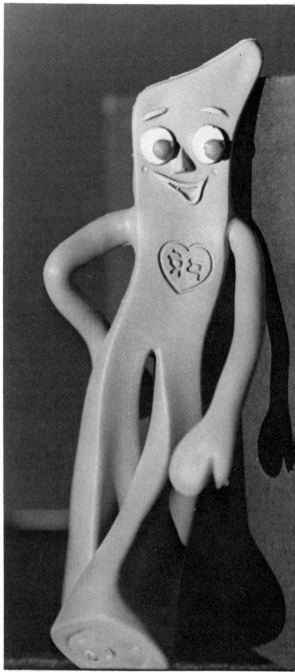

*Gumby*: The popular hero. (Courtesy of Art
Clokey.)

*Heckle and Jeckel*: The inseparable crows. (Courtesy of Viacom International, Inc.)

## THE HECKLE AND JECKLE SHOW

*Saturday, 11:00–11:30 a.m.: CBS*
*Debut: 10/14/56; Cancellation; 9/8/57 (CBS)*
*Return: 1/25/58; Cancellation: 9/24/60 (CBS)*
*Return: 9/25/65; Cancellation: 9/3/66 (CBS)*
*Return: 9/6/69; Cancellation: 9/4/71 (NBC)*

*Supplier: Terrytoons*
*Voice characterizations: Paul Frees*

Heckle and Jeckle were two extremely talkative and simple-minded magpies, never able to make up their minds without fussing over the consequences. Invariably, after weighing the pros and cons of a situation, they would make the worst possible decision. This comical situation made the series one of the most popular cartoons on network television.

Produced by Terrytoons studios, one of the oldest animation houses, the cartoon originated in the 1940s in a series of shorts shown in movie theaters. The pair had made their debut on television on the *CBS Cartoon Theater*, hosted by Dick Van Dyke. The show also featured other Terrytoons characters, including Dinky Duck, Gandy Goose, Little Roquefort (the trouble-making mouse), Percy the Cat, and The Terry Bears.

Since the 1950s these magpies have been seen all over the world, and their images appear on a variety of tie-in merchandise. They have also been seen on *Claude Kirschner's Terry Tell Time* series. The cartoons continue to appear in syndication on local stations.

*Ruff and Reddy:* The stars. (Courtesy of Hanna-Barbera Productions.)

## HI, MOM!

**Saturday,** *9:00 – 10:00 a.m.: NBC*
**Debut:** *9/15/57;* **Cancellation:** *3/20/59*
**Hostess:** *Shari Lewis*

Shari Lewis was seen here in an unfamiliar role, playing hostess to a show for the young mother. The program consisted of advice from guests, interspersed with entertainment for young women who were housebound with new infants. As usual, Shari was accompanied by her puppets, Lamb Chop, Charlie Horse and Hush Puppy.

## THE PAUL WINCHELL SHOW

**Sunday,** *5:30 – 6:00 p.m.: ABC*
**Debut:** *9/29/57;* **Cancellation:** *4/3/60*
**Producer:** *Paul Winchell*

This was the fifth network series for ventriloquist Paul Winchell and his wooden companion, Jerry Mahoney. They were supported by comedian Frank Fontaine and musician Milton DeLugg. The variety format, similar to Winchell's previous shows, featured comedy sketches. (See also: **Winchell and Mahoney** (1947/48) and **Dunninger and Winchell** (1948/49).

# RUFF AND REDDY SHOW

*Saturday, 10:30 – 11:00 a.m.: NBC*
*Debut: 12/14/57; Cancellation: 9/26/64*
*Supplier: Hanna-Barbera Productions*
*Hosts: Jimmy Blaine, Bob Cottle*

### Voices
Ruff . . . . . . . . . . . . . . . . . . . . . .*Don Messick*
Reddy . . . . . . . . . . . . . . . . . . .*Daws Butler*

This animated series, created by Joseph Barbera and Bill Hanna, was the famous team's first television cartoon.

Ruff was a quick-thinking cat, and Reddy was his lovable but not-so-bright canine friend. The premise of this highly successful show was the friendship of two creatures commonly thought to be enemies. Through their zany adventures, fearful and fearsome, the series explored the compatibility of these cartoon animals.

Barbera and Hanna left MGM in 1957, where they had made a substantial number of theatrical cartoons. They are remembered as the producers and directors of the award-winning *Tom and Jerry* cartoons, a favorite on the big screen, and, later, on weekly television. Joseph Barbera, a New Yorker, met William Hanna, a New Mexican, while they were at MGM. Barbera had first worked for the Van Beuren studio, and Hanna for Harman-Ising before coming to Metro, where they spent the next 20 years. The Hanna-Barbera studio has produced more television cartoons than any other, and it has received numerous awards for its many successes. The studio's *Flintstones* was the longest running prime-time cartoon in television history. *Ruff and Reddy* was the springboard for the team's momentous TV success.

# SHARILAND

*Saturday, 8:00 – 9:00 a.m.: NBC*
*Debut: 3/16/57; Cancellation: Summer 1957*
*Hostess: Shari Lewis*

This children's variety series was hosted by ventriloquist Shari Lewis, accompanied by her inimitable puppets, Lamb Chop, Charlie Horse and Hush Puppy. But it was with **The Shari Lewis Show** (1960/61) that she really attained success.

*Shariland*: Shari Lewis and Lamb Chop. (Courtesy of Shari Lewis.)

1958 - 1959 Season

# SHIRLEY TEMPLE'S STORY BOOK

*Monday, 7:30–8:30 p.m.: ABC*
*Sunday, 7:00–8:00 p.m.: NBC*
*Debut: 1/12/59; Cancellation: 12/59 (ABC)*
*Return: 9/60; Cancellation: 9/10/61 (NBC)*
*Executive Producer: William H. Brown, Jr.*
*Producer: William Asher*
*Hostess: Shirley Temple*

Shirley Temple, the fondly remembered, curly-haired screen tot of the 1930s, hosted this prime-time family entertainment. Ms. Temple also made guest dramatic appearances and provided the narration for such children's classics as A. A. Milne's *Winnie The Pooh, Babes in Toyland, The Reluctant Dragon* and *The Prince and The Pauper*. A number of established actors and actresses, including Charlton Heston, Jonathan Winters, Agnes Moorehead and Claire Bloom appeared on the show, which was launched in 1958 as a series of 16 prime-time specials. The following year it aired every third week, alternating with the hit Western series, *Cheyenne*. In 1960, the program was transferred to NBC and renamed *The Shirley Temple Show*.

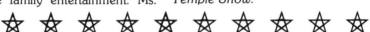

# THE UNCLE AL SHOW

*Saturday, 11:00–12:00 noon: ABC*
*Debut: 10/18/58; Cancellation: 9/19/59*
*Producers: Al and Wanda Lewis*
*Puppeteer: Larry Smith*

*Uncle Al*: Uncle Al and his accordion. (Courtesy of Al Lewis.)

## Cast

Uncle Al .................*Al Lewis*
Cinderella ...............*Janet Green*
Captain Windy ...........*Wanda Lewis*

Each week 40 children of varying ages were selected from thousands applying to participate in *The Uncle Al Show,* which stressed traditional moral values and the importance of good health. They assisted Uncle Al in acting out mini-dramas. Lewis, an accomplished guitar and banjo player, provided spontaneous musical fillers, often with his accordion. Each sketch lasted 60 to 90 seconds, and a number of puppets participated.

The show continues to this day on local station WCPO in Cincinnati. The moral values taught in the late 1950s are still emphasized, although the format is more sophisticated now.

*Uncle Al:* Uncle Al and his young audience. (Courtesy of Al Lewis.)

# MATTY'S FUNDAY FUNNIES

*Sunday, 5:00–5:30 p.m.: ABC*
*Friday, 7:30–8:00 p.m.: ABC*
*Debut: 10/11/59; Cancellation: 12/29/62*
*Supplier: Harvey Films*

Mattel, the toy manufacturer, was the sponsor of this collection of animated cartoons, conceived as an extension of the Sunday newspaper comic strips. The hosts were the cartoon characters, Matty and Sisterbelle. The cartoons were all reruns of old Harvey material, originally distributed by Paramount.

Other pen-and-ink stars were Casper, the Friendly Ghost, Baby Huey, the mischievous overgrown duckling; Little Audrey; Buzzy the crow; Tommy Turtle; and Katnip and Herman.

In 1961 the series underwent a major change at the hands of the innovative Bob Clampett. Many of the same characters would later appear in ***Beany and Cecil*** (1961/62).

© HARVEY FAMOUS CARTOONS

---

*Matty's Sunday Funnies*: A hare and a tortoise. (Courtesy of Harvey Productions Inc.)

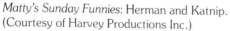

*Matty's Sunday Funnies:* Herman and Katnip. (Courtesy of Harvey Productions Inc.)

*Matty's Sunday Funnies:* Baby Huey and a friend. (Courtesy of Harvey Productions Inc.)

*Matty's Sunday Funnies:* Casper, Herman, Katnip, Baby Huey, Little Audrey and Buzzy the Crow. (Courtesy of Harvey Productions Inc.)

*Matty's Sunday Funnies:* Casper, Baby Huey, Little Audrey, Herman and Katnip. (Courtesy of Harvey Productions Inc.)

1960-1961 Season

© Warner Bros. Inc. 1980

Printed in U.S.A.    BB-4-B   12/80

*Bugs Bunny Show*: Bugs Bunny on the move. (Courtesy of Warner Communications, Inc.)

## THE BUGS BUNNY SHOW

*Tuesday, 7:30 – 8:00 p.m.: ABC*
*Debut: 10/11/60; Cancellation: 9/25/62*
*Supplier: Warner Brothers*
*Voices: Mel Blanc*

"Eh-h-h-h . . . What's Up, Doc?" This is the trademark rhetorical question proffered by the world-famous smart-aleck rabbit, Bugs Bunny.

The character was spawned in the 1930s, as a competitor to Walt Disney's *Mickey Mouse*. Jack Warner, head of Warner Brothers, contacted Leon Schlessinger's infant animation studio to come up with an equally popular character. Schlessinger employed many leading animators, some of whom had grown disenchanted with Disney's operation and were looking for new opportunities. Among them were Fritz Freleng, one of the greatest animation directors of all time. Freleng created *Porky Pig* (1934), *Yosemite Sam* and *Sylvester, the cat* (1944). He also contributed significantly to *Daffy Duck* (1937). But his greatest creation, in collaboration with Tex Avery, was *Bugs Bunny* (1939).

Bugs Bunny appeared in movies for over 20 years. With the dramatic growth of television and the networks' constant need for inexpensive material, Warner saw the opportunity of turning a profit from its old inventory. Entering into an arrangement with ABC, the studio repackaged and released to television all of its movie cartoons.

Many writers worked on the cartoons over the years, including Ted Pierce, Mike Maltese and Warren Foster. Directors included Chuck Jones and Bob McKimson, the originator of *Foghorn, the Leghorn* and *The Tasmanian Devil.* After leaving Warner's, Chuck Jones worked on *Tom and Jerry* at MGM with Bill Hanna and Joe Barbera. He also contributed to such TV cartoon specials as *Horton Hears a Who, The Grinch,* a Dr. Seuss adaptation, *Raggedy Ann and Andy* and the Saturday morning series, *Curiosity Shop.* Bob Clampett has contributed to many shows since being at Warner's, which he left to create **Beany and Cecil** (1961/62). In 1962 Fritz Freleng formed a partnership with David DePatie to produce animated specials and Saturday programs. These included **The Pink Panther** (1969/70) and *The Oddball Couple.* The company disbanded, and Freleng has since joined Hanna–Barbera.

---

*Bugs Bunny Show* : Bugs taking it easy. (Courtesy of Warner Communications, Inc.)

# THE FLINTSTONES

*Friday, 8:30–9:00 p.m.: ABC*
*Debut: 9/30/60; Cancellation: 9/2/66*
*Supplier: Hanna-Barbera Productions*

*Voices:*

Fred Flintstone . . . . . . . . *Alan Reed,*
*Henry Corden*
Wilma Flintstone . . . . . . *Jean VanderPyl*
Barney Rubble . . . . . . . . *Mel Blanc*
Betty Rubble . . . . . . . . . *Bea Benaderet*
*(1960–1964),*
*Gerry Johnson*
*(1964–1966)*
Dino . . . . . . . . . . . . . . . *Mel Blanc*
Pebbles Flintstone . . . . . . *Jean VanderPyle*
Bamm-Bamm Rubble . . . *Don Messick*
Mr. Slate . . . . . . . . . . . . . *John Stephenson*
The Great Kazoo . . . . . . . *Harvey Corman*

The Flintstones was inspired by comedian Jackie Gleason's memorable prime-time series, *The Honeymooners*. Bill Hanna and Joe Barbera turned back the clock and set their animated reconstruction in a prehistoric suburb of Neanderthal America.

Fred and Wilma were much like Ralph and Alice Kramden. (Their daughter, Pebbles, entered the program in 1962.) Their next-door neighbors, Barney and Betty Rubble, were similar to the Nortons. They had a baby son, Bamm-Bamm, who's most enjoyable pastime was pounding the floor with a club. His immense strength could cause earth tremors.

Fred worked at the Rock Head & Quarry Cave Construction Company, as the operator of a dinosaur-powered crane. He was usually at odds with his boss, Mr. Slate. Like Ralph Kramden, Fred was always attempting to improve his lot. He endured the trials and tribulations of work, marriage and friendship, all the while attempting to make ends meet. Just as Ralph and Ed belonged to the "Raccoon Lodge," Fred and Barney were members of the "Royal Order of Water Buffalos," a collection of hard-working husbands who just wanted a few hours away from their nagging spouses.

In addition to their brilliant parody of suburban life, Hanna and Barbera were innovative in their use of unexpected sight gags. For instance, a pelican used its large bill as a waste receptacle, a turtle became a lampshade, a small elephant used its trunk as a vacuum cleaner, and so forth.

The series spawned **Pebbles and Bamm-Bamm** (1971/72), featuring the adolescent Flintstone and Rubble children. Since its prime-time run, *The Flintstones* has appeared in syndication throughout the world. The program has won awards for animation and innovation, including Fame's Annual Critics' Poll as the most unique new program, and the Golden Globe for outstanding achievement in international television cartoons. Merchandising tie-ins have continued for over two decades, with *Flintstones* comic books, toys, lunch boxes, breakfast cereals, soap and even vitamins.

*The Flintstones* was the longest running prime-time cartoon series in television history.

---

*The Flintstones*: Dino, the family pet. (Courtesy of Hanna-Barbera Productions.)

*The Flintstones*: The Great Kazoo. (Courtesy of Hanna-Barbera Productions.)

*The Flintstones*: Barney Rubble. (Courtesy of Hanna-Barbera Productions.)

*The Flintstones*: Betty Rubble. (Courtesy of Hanna-Barbera Productions.)

*The Flintstones*: Wilma Flintstone. (Courtesy of Hanna-Barbera Productions.)

*The Flintstones*: Fred Flintstone. (Courtesy of Hanna-Barbera Productions.)

*The Flintstones*: Pebbles and Bamm-Bamm. (Courtesy of Hanna-Barbera Productions.)

## KING LEONARDO AND HIS SHORT SUBJECTS

**Saturday,** *10:30–11:00 a.m.: NBC*
**Debut:** *10/15/60; Cancellation: 9/28/63*
**Supplier:** *TOTAL-Television, Leonardo Productions Inc.*

### Voices

King Leonardo . . . . . . . . . .*Jackson Beck*
Odie Colognie . . . . . . . . . . .*Allan Swift*
Itchy Brother . . . . . . . . . . . .*Allan Swift*
Biggy Rat . . . . . . . . . . . . . . .*Jackson Beck*
Tooter Turtle . . . . . . . . . . . .*Allan Swift*
Lizard, the Wizard  . . . . . . .*Frank Milano*
The Hunter . . . . . . . . . . . . .*Kenny Delmar*

This animated series took place in the land of Bongo Congo, deep in the African jungle, Its majestic yet vulnerable ruler was a lion called King Leonardo. Fortunately for King Leo, his trusted aide Odie Colognie (a comical skunk), was on hand to intercede when terror struck in the form of Biggy Rat, Leo's sworn enemy. The rat wanted to replace Leo on the throne with Leo's villainous brother, Itchy Brother.

The show was divided into three segments. The other two were called *Tooter Turtle* and *The Hunter*.

Tooter invoked the magic powers of a lizard called Mr. Wizard to change himself into different characters or objects. Unfortunately, his plans often went awry, requiring swift intervention from Mr. Wizard.

Contrary to the myth of the resourceful,

*King Leonardo and his Short Subjects*: The Hunter, The Fox, Horrors Hunter and Flim Flanagan. (Courtesy of Leonardo-TTV Productions.)

efficient bloodhound as tracker, the Hunter is an incompetent detective. To make matters worse, his young nephew, Horrors, invariably uncovers the clues that lead the hapless Hunter on a continuing search to apprehend the notorious Fox.

NBC dropped the series in 1963, but the individual episodes were subsequently integrated into other TOTAL-Television cartoon formats. In syndication *King Leonardo* was known as *The King and Odie,* and the cartoon became part of **Tennessee Tuxedo and His Tales** (1963/64). *Tooter Turtle* also turned up in *Tennessee Tuxedo.* Horrors, the Hunter and Officer Flim Flanagan were later to be seen in **Underdog** (1964/65).

*King Leonardo and His Short Subjects* was the first cartoon produced by TOTAL, in partnership with Leonardo Productions. It was sponsored by General Mills, an association formulated by their agency, Dancer Fitzgerald Sample.

TOTAL, formed in 1959, combined the talents of writers Buck Biggers and Chet Stover, art director/designer Joe Harris, and sound recordist Treadwell Covington. The *Leonardo* project was headed by Peter Peach, who at the time was also involved in a live series entitled *Pip, The Piper.*

The company sought out actors whose voices most perfectly suited the cartoon characters. Wally Cox enacted Underdog. Kenny Delmar, who had worked in radio playing Senator Klaghorn in *Allan's Alley,* had so impressed Treadwell Covington that the character of the Hunter was created and developed to conform with Delmar's comedy style.

Although TOTAL-Television no longer produces programs, their productions are in syndication all over the world. Their characters still appear in merchandising tie-ins.

*King Leonardo and his Short Subjects* (clockwise from top right): Odie Colognie, King Leonardo's suave prime minister; Itchy Brother, the scheming brother of the King; Biggy Rat, his accomplice; and King Leonard. (Courtesy of Leonardo-TTV Productions.)

# THE MAGIC LAND OF ALLAKAZAM

*Saturday,* 11:00 – 11:30 a.m.: CBS
*Debut:* 10/1/60; *Cancellation:* 9/22/62
  (CBS)
*Return:* 9/29/62; *Cancellation:* 12/28/63

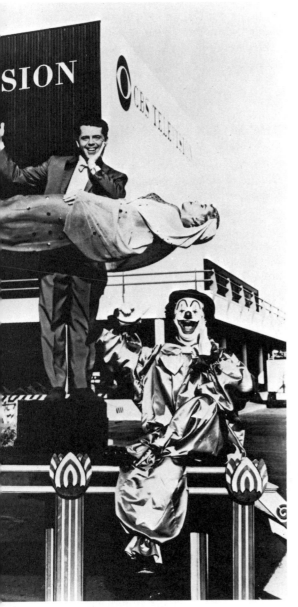

(ABC)
*Return:* 4/25/64; *Cancellation:* 12/12/64
  (ABC)
*Producers:* Mark Wilson, Jack Whipper,
  Dan Whitman
*Host:* Mark Wilson

*Cast*
Mark Wilson . . . . . . . . . . . . .Himself
Nani Darnell . . . . . . . . . . . . .Herself
Mike Wilson . . . . . . . . . . . . .Himself
Rebo the clown . . . . . . . . .Bev Bergerson
The King of Allakazam . . . .Bob Towner
Perriwinkle . . . . . . . . . . . . . .Chuck Barnes
*Other players:* Jackie Joseph, Bob Fenton

Set in the magical land of Allakazam, this
series starred professional illusionist Mark
Wilson as a magician who used the tricks of
his trade to outwit such nasty characters as
"Evilo." Wilson was accompanied by his
wife Nani and their son, Mike. The family
operated puppets, including Basil the Baf-
fling Bunny, Doris the Daring Dove, Charles
the Charming Chicken, and Bernard, the
Biggest Bunny in the Business.

  The program had its genesis in *Time for
Magic,* a program Wilson packaged and sold
to ABC's Dallas affiliate WFAA in 1954. The
show's popularity spread throughout Texas,
where it was carried regionally. In August,
1960, Kellogg's bought the show and sold it
to the CBS network under its sponsorship as
*The Magic Land of Allakazam.*

  During its first year on the network, the
series aired previously broadcast Hanna-
Barbera cartoons, including *Huckleberry
Hound, Yogi Bear,* and *Pixie and Dixie.*
After the show's second season, these car-
toons were no longer shown.

  Since the demise of *Allakazam,* Wilson
has operated his own production and merchandising business. He has staged magic
acts for many films and television series, including *Wonder Woman, The Six Million
Dollar Man, Columbo* and *The Love Boat.*

*Magic Land of Allakazam*: Mark Wilson, his
wife, Nani Darnell, and Rebo, the clown. (Courtesy of Mark Wilson.)

# PIP THE PIPER

*Saturday and Sunday, 11:30 – 12:00 noon:*
    *ABC*
*Saturday, 9:30 – 10:00 a.m.: NBC*
*Debut: 12/5/60; Cancellation: 5/28/61*
    *(ABC)*
*Return: 6/24/61; Cancellation: 9/22/62*
    *(NBC)*
*Executive Producer: Peter Peach*
*Producer: Jack Miller*

*Cast*
Pip, the Piper . . . . . . . . . .Jack Spear
Miss Merrynote . . . . . . . .Phyllis Spear
Mr. Leader . . . . . . . . . . .Lucien Kaminsky

Jack Spear and Lucien Kaminsky created and wrote episodes for this live show, which combined the whimsical qualities of Peter Pan and The Pied Piper of Hamelin.

Spear and his partner presented an idea for this show to Peter Peach, at that time head of Producers' Associates of Television (PAT), in New York.

Pip, first cousin to Peter Pan and half-brother to the Pied Piper, was dressed as a medieval minstrel and played a magic flute. Episodes were set in the magic land of Pipertown, a utopian hamlet in the clouds where the necessities of life grew on trees and nothing needed to be manufactured. Whenever anything was needed all a character had to do was "reach for a tree"—a flute tree, or a piano tree, for example.

Like James M. Barrie's Peter Pan, Pip would float up to his magic and musical hideaway. Accompanied by Miss Merrynote and Mr. Leader, Pip engaged in all manner of wonderful adventures. Music was a universal language in Pipertown, where every citizen conversed by playing a musical instrument. Mr. Leader (Lucien Kaminsky) co-ordinated the citizens' "conversation" and played many of the roles. All the women resembled Miss Merrynote (for obvious reasons), who wore a "Miss Pennypocket" skirt with a piano key design. Pip possessed no wings, so a mode of transportation was de-vised that could move the hero to and from the magic land. Jack Spear would stand on an eight foot board that had been painted blue to simulate the sky. Dry ice was thrown into buckets of boiling water and a fan turned on. Then a magnetized cut-out model of Pip would be drawn upwards through the 'steam' towards the ceiling, giving the impression of the piper in flight. For in-flight close-ups Spear would be moved about the studio on a dolly against the blue background.

# THE SHARI LEWIS SHOW

*Saturday, 10:00 – 10:30 a.m.: NBC*
*Debut: 10/1/60; Cancellation: 9/28/63*
*Producer: Robert Scherer*
*Hostess: Shari Lewis*

*Regular performers:*
Mr. Goodfellow . . . . . . . . . Ronald Redd
Jump Pup . . . . . . . . . . . . . . Jackie Warner

Ventriloquist Shari Lewis hosted this children's variety show, which featured her popular puppets, Lamb Chop, Charlie Horse and Hush Puppy. Shari was often visited by Jump Pup, a Saint Bernard, and Mr. Goodfellow, a kindly neighbor.

Ms. Lewis acted out stories, sang songs and chatted with her puppet friends. Various guest stars appeared on the show over the years, including Ossie Davis, Bill Hayes, Jerry Orbach and Clive Revill. Dom DeLuise made his television debut here and appeared regularly. Music played a major role in the show, with an average of six songs per episode. The lyrics and musical arrangements were by Lan O'Kun.

Intended to be educational but fun, episodes contained simple stories about overcoming fear and phobias, learning to use reason and the like.

Other shows featuring or hosted by Shari

*Pip, the Piper* (left to right): Mr. Leader, Pip and Miss Merrynote. (Courtesy of Jack Spear.)

Lewis include **Shariland** (1957/58) and **Hi Mom** (1957/58).

Before working in television Ms. Lewis had perfected her art as assistant to her father—"Peter Pan, the Magic Man," appearing with him at performances in New York. She is an accomplished writer and has authored a number of books for children. Saul Turtletaub, chief writer for the show, went on to produce *The New Dick Van Dyke Show, Sanford and Son, What's Happening,* and *Carter Country,* among others. He has maintained an interest in children's programming and is now a partner in the TOY Productions Company.

1961-1962 Season

# THE ALVIN SHOW

*Wednesday, 7:30 – 8:00 p.m.: CBS*
*Debut: 10/4/61; Cancellation: 9/5/62 (CBS)*
*Return: 3/10/79; Cancellation: 9/1/79 (NBC)*
*Supplier: Herbert Klein and The Bagdasarian Film Corp.*

## Voices

Alvin . . . . . . . . . . . . . . . .Ross Bagdasarian
Theodore . . . . . . . . . . . . .Ross Bagdasarian
Simon . . . . . . . . . . . . . . .Ross Bagdasarian
David Seville . . . . . . . . . .Ross Bagdasarian
Clyde Crashcup  . . . . . . .Shepard Menken
Sinbad . . . . . . . . . . . . . . Tim Matthieson
Salty . . . . . . . . . . . . . . . .Mel Blanc
**Other voices:** *June Foray, Lee Patrick, Bill Lee, William Sanford, Res Dennis*

*The Alvin Show* derived from a 1958 novelty record titled *The Chipmunk Song,* which sold over four million copies. The recording artist, Ross Bagdasarian (stage name David Seville), conjured up this group of singing cartoon chipmunks for a television series. Chipmunks Theodore and Simon were beyond reproach, but their brother, Alvin, was a problem child. He was the lead singer and the most mischievous of the lot, forever exasperating his mentor. The chipmunks' voices were created by running voice tracks at exaggerated speeds to provide a high-pitched falsetto harmony.

The television series was concerned with the group's antics and Bagdasarian's inevitable remonstrances. There was usually at least one musical interlude in each half hour. In addition, there were two regular cartoon segments. *The Adventures of Clyde Crashcup* concerned a deranged professor who took credit for the invention of any and all objects mentioned in the episode. He always paid a heavy price for assuming the responsibility. *Sinbad, Jr.* featured the "thrilling" adventures of a sailor and his parrot companion, Salty.

Ross Bagdasarian retired from show bus-iness in 1967. In June 1980, Excelsior Records released a new album, "Chipmunk Punk," which became a children's hit. It was followed by "Urban Chipmunk," another hit in 1981. In the fall of that same year came yet another success—"A Chipmunk Christmas." In excess of $18 million was netted from these three albums. Ross's son, Ross, Jr., has continued to operate his father's company. The incorrigible Alvin and his brothers were seen on a prime-time TV special in 1981.

Alvin and the chipmunks will return to Saturday morning television in September 1983.

# BEANY AND CECIL

*Saturday, 7:00 – 7:30 p.m.: ABC*
*Debut: 1/6/62; Cancellation: 12/19/64*
*Creator/Producer: Bob Clampett*
*Voices: Erv Shoemaker, Jim McGeorge, Walker Edmonston, Eddie Berandt, Mickey Katz*

This program had its genesis in *Time for Beany,* which debuted on February 28, 1949, over KTLA, in Los Angeles. It featured two puppets, Beany and Cecil. Beany was a little boy with a propellor-topped cap, and Cecil, his pet and his constant companion, was a seasick sea serpent. Daws Butler and Stan Freberg, respectively, provided the voices of Beany and Cecil. Additional characters were spoken by Jerry Colonna. A 15-minute show, *Beany and Cecil* won critical acclaim from kids and adults, in addition to Emmy Awards in 1949, 1950 and 1952.

Clampett, a former newspaper cartoonist, had worked for Warner Brothers Cartoons from 1931 to 1946, where he helped animate Bugs Bunny. While there, he created Tweety Pie, one of that studio's most successful cartoon characters. In 1959, Clampett turned Beany and Cecil into animated cartoon characters for their appearance in *Matty's Funday Funnies,* sponsored by Mattel Toys. In January, 1962, the series went network, retitled *Matty's Funnies with Beany and Cecil*. It was soon abbreviated to *Beany and Cecil*.

Beany and Captain Huffenpuff spent much of their time aboard their ship, the Leakin' Lena, sailing in and out of trouble. They met such unprepossessing foes as Dishonest John, Homer, the Octopus, Tear-a-Long, the Dotted Lion, and Carless, the Mexican Hairless. Characters that survived from the *Time for Beany* days were Louie, the Lone Shark, and Dizzy Lou, the Kangaroo.

## THE BULLWINKLE SHOW

*Sunday, 7:00–7:30 p.m.: NBC*
*Debut: 9/24/61; Cancellation: 9/15/63 (NBC)*
*Return: 9/21/63; Cancellation: 9/5/64 (NBC)*
*Return: 9/20/64; Cancellation: 9/2/73 (ABC)*
*Producer: Bill Scott*
*Supplier: Jay Ward Productions*
*Narrators: William Conrad, Edward Everett Horton*

*Voices*
Bullwinkle . . . . . . . . . . . . . . *Bill Scott*
Rocky . . . . . . . . . . . . . . . . *June Foray*
Boris Badenov . . . . . . . . . . *Paul Frees*
Natasha Fataly . . . . . . . . . *June Foray*
Aesop . . . . . . . . . . . . . . . . *Charles Ruggles*
Peabody . . . . . . . . . . . . . . *Bill Scott*
Sherman . . . . . . . . . . . . . . *Walter Tetley*
Dudley Do-Right . . . . . . . . *Bill Scott*
Snidely Whiplash . . . . . . . . *Hans Conreid*
**Other voices:** Skip Craig, Barbara Baldwin, Adrienne Diamond

This popular show was essentially a retitled version of ***Rocky and his Friends*** (1959/60).

Bullwinkle, the moose, was again accompanied by Rocky, the impish flying

*The Alvin Show*: Alvin, Theodore and Simon. (Courtesy of Bagdasarian Film Corp.)

squirrel with a big grin and a pilot's cap. Together, they defeated the wicked schemes of Mr. Big, a midget with grand ideas. Big's Russian-agent colleagues were Boris Bad-enov ("long for Bad") and Natasha Fataly ("long for fatal"). See the entry for **Rocky and His Friends** (1959/60) for specific information on this show.

*Beany and Cecil:* Cecil the seasick serpent, Beany Boy and Captain Huff'n'Puff. (Courtesy of Bob Clampett.)

*The Bullwinkle Show*: Bullwinkle, the moose. (Courtesy of P.A.T./Ward Productions.)

## CALVIN AND THE COLONEL

*Tuesday, 8:30–9:00 p.m.: ABC*
*Debut: 10/3/61; Cancellation: 9/22/62*
*Producers: Freeman Gosden and Charles Correll for Kayro Productions*

### Voices
The Colonel . . . . . . . . . . *Freeman Gosden*
Calvin . . . . . . . . . . . . . . . *Charles Correll*
Maggie Belle . . . . . . . . . *Virginia Gregg*
Sister Sue . . . . . . . . . . . . *Beatrice Kay*
Oliver Wendell Clutch . . . *Paul Frees*

Freeman Gosden and Charles Correll had been famous during the 1930s and 1940s for their long-running radio series, *Amos 'N' Andy*, a comedy depicting the misadventures of a pair of black men. Such racial stereotypes were no longer permitted on the airwaves by the 1960s, however.

So Correll and Gosden, both white, created and supplied voices for this animated cartoon series, which was essentially *Amos' N' Andy* in a less controversial format. The show centered on the friendship of a sly

*Calvin and the Colonel*: Colonel Montgomery  J. Klaxton (left), and Calvin Burnside. (Courtesy of Universal City Studios, Inc.)

fox and a simple bear. The animals moved to the industrial North from the deep South, with resultant discomforts, supposedly due to their ignorance and a lack of adaptability. The Colonel (the fox) was accompanied by his wife, Maggie Belle and her sister. Weasel Wendell Clutch, a lawyer, usually exacerbated the difficulties the two brought upon themselves.

The show has been syndicated by MCA since leaving ABC.

## MAGIC RANCH

*Saturday, 11:00 – 11:30 a.m.: ABC*
*Debut: 9/30/61; Cancellation: 12/17/61*
*Producer: George Anderson*
*Host: Don Alan*

This magic series had the distinction of being set on a dude ranch—a ranch operated solely for the entertainment of tourists. Host Don Alan, an accomplished magician dressed in a cowboy outfit, performed tricks and introduced guest acts. These were usually established illusionists and "first-time-out" junior magicians. Asian Indian illusionists, "black arts" magicians, and even comedy magic acts appeared on the show.

The series emanated from ABC's Chicago affiliate WNER (now WLS-TV) and ran for 13 weeks.

*Magic Ranch*: Don Alan on the set. (Courtesy of   Theodore Schulte.)

*1, 2, 3, Go!*
Richard Thomas.
(Courtesy of Jack
Kuney.)

## 1,2,3,GO

*Sunday, 6:30 – 7:00 p.m.: NBC*
*Debut: 10/8/61; Cancellation: 5/27/62*
*Producer: Jack Kuney*

This series attempted to teach civics and career counseling to junior high-age children. Its exploratory format attempted to portray the excitement of discovery. Hosts Jack Lescoulie and 10-year-old Richard Thomas learned about society and the functions of its myriad members.

Programs included visits to NASA headquarters in Houston, the Treasury Department in Washington, D.C. and an Eskimo village in Alaska. The pair interviewed such Government figures as William O. Douglas,

*Top Cat*: Top Cat (with pointer) and the Gang ' with Officer Dibble, the bane of T.C.'s existence. (Courtesy of Hanna-Barbera Productions.)

the Supreme Court Justice, and Robert F. Kennedy, the Attorney General.

Richard Thomas has since forged a strong show business career for himself. He played John Boy on CBS's prime-time drama *The Waltons,* and has had roles on Broadway, in television and film.

## TOP CAT

**Wednesday,** *8:30–9:00 p.m.: ABC*
**Debut:** *9/27/61;* **Cancellation:** *9/26/62* (*ABC*)
**Return:** *10/6/62;* **Cancellation:** *3/30/63* (*ABC*)
**Return:** *4/3/65;* **Cancellation:** *12/31/66* (*NBC*)
**Supplier:** *Hanna-Barbera Productions*

## Voices

| | |
|---|---|
| Top Cat (T.C.) . . . . . . . . | Arnold Stang |
| Benny the Ball . . . . . . . . | Maurice Gosfield |
| Choo-Choo . . . . . . . . . . | Marvin Kaplan |
| Spook . . . . . . . . . . . . . . . | Leo De Lyon |
| The Brain . . . . . . . . . . . . | Leo De Lyon |
| Fancy Fancy . . . . . . . . . . | John Stephenson |
| Goldie . . . . . . . . . . . . . . . | Jean VanderPyl |
| Pierre . . . . . . . . . . . . . . . | John Stephenson |
| Officer Dibble . . . . . . . . . | Allen Jenkins |

*Other voices:* Paul Frees

Top Cat—T.C. to his friends—was a sly con artist and the leader of a pack of Broadway alley cats. T.C. and his gang lived among the street's overflowing trash cans, all the while complaining about the accommodations. They made their phone calls from the police call box at the corner and collected their meals from the back of the neighborhood deli. Milk and reading matter came from people's doorsteps. They were a thoroughly antisocial bunch.

For a gang of alley cats, they seemed to have organized matters well, except for one minor irritation—overzealous police officer Dibble. This upright defender of peace and quiet was the avowed enemy of the hobo felines. He expended much courage, energy and determination in unsuccessful attempts to secure an indictment against them.

1962-1963 Season

*The Jetsons:* The entire family, left to right: Elroy, Judy, George, Jane and Astro. (Courtesy of Hanna-Barbera Productions.)

# CARTOONSVILLE

*Saturday, 11:00–11:30 a.m.: ABC*
*Debut: 4/6/63; Cancellation: 9/28/63*
*Host: Paul Winchell*

Paul Winchell, accompanied by his puppets Jerry Mahoney and Knucklehead Smith, provided the continuity for these animated cartoons. All were first-run and made after 1958. These included *Scatt Skitt, Sheriff Saddle Head* and *Goodie the Gremlin*.

For additional information on Winchell, see the entries on the **Winchell and Mahoney Show** (1947/48), **Dunninger and Winchell** (1948/49), the **Paul Winchell–Jerry Mahoney Show** (1950/51), **Jerry Mahoney Club House** (1954/55) and the **Paul Winchell Show** (1957/58).

# THE JETSONS

*Sunday, 7:30–8:00 p.m.: ABC*
*Debut: 9/23/62; Cancellation: 9/8/63*
*Supplier: Hanna-Barbera Productions*

*Voices*
George Jetson . . . . . . . .George O'Hanlon
Jane Jetson . . . . . . . . . . .Penny Singleton
Judy Jetson . . . . . . . . . .Janet Waldo
Elroy Jetson . . . . . . . . . .Daws Butler
Astro . . . . . . . . . . . . . . .Don Messick
Cosmo G.
    Spacely . . . . . . . . . . .Mel Blanc
*Other voices: Howard Morris, Herschel Bernardi, Howard McNear, Frank Nelson*

The Jetsons was a space-age version of Hanna-Barbera's highly successful animated cartoon, **The Flintstones** (1960/61), which was inspired by the prime-time live-action series, The Honeymooners.

The setting was 21st-century middle-class America. A young family, the Jetsons, lived in an ultramodern "skypad" apartment equipped with every imaginable and unimaginable domestic aid and creature comfort. These included a robot maid and an electronic device to move the apartment in the event of bad weather. Episodes concerned such day-to-day problems as commuting, school work, job pressures and evening meal decisions. The series was conceived of as a parody of contemporary suburban life.

Although the series lasted only briefly on prime time, it enjoyed a long and prosperous run on Saturday mornings. It has since gone into syndication.

# MAGIC MIDWAY

*Saturday, 11:30–12:00 noon: NBC*
*Debut: 9/22/62; Cancellation: 3/16/63*
*Producers: Jack Miller and James Shaw*
*Host: Claude Kirchner*
*Regulars: Bill Bailey, Lou Stein, Bonnie Lee, Phil Kiley, Douglas Anderson*

Claude Kirchner, host of the successful 1950s' series **Super Circus** (1948/49), returned to network television as ringmaster of this circus extravaganza. Accompanying Kirchner were Bonnie Lee, a baton-twirling majorette, circus performers "Boom-Boom" Bailey and "Coo-Coo" Kiley and "Mr. Pocus" Anderson, a magician. The music was supplied by the jazz band of Lou Stein and the Circus Seven.

Kirchner, originally a radio personality, had been a spokesperson for Marx Toys by Marx since 1958. *Magic Midway* was conceived as a vehicle to promote their products—a variation on the Kirchner success formula of the 1950s. The toy company was the sole sponsor for the first 13 weeks, but its executives grew to dislike the format, clearing the way for open advertising until the show's cancellation. Kirchner returned to radio, and he remains based in Chicago. Producer Jack Miller was a co-creator of *Captain Kangaroo*.

*Magic Midway:* Claude Kirchner and Clownie. (Courtesy of Claude Kirchner.)

## PICTURE THIS

*Tuesday, 9:30–10:00 p.m.: CBS*
*Debut: 6/25/63; Cancellation: 9/17/63*
*Producers: Ben Joelson, Art Baer*

This game show was hosted by Jerry Van Dyke, Dick's brother. It offered two competing teams, each comprised of a celebrity and a member of the audience. One member of each team was given a phrase, which was concealed from his partner. The player would suggest clues for the "artist" to draw and thus identify the phrase. The first team with the correct answer received cash prizes.

After serving his apprenticeship in night clubs, comedian Van Dyke made several appearances on his brother's series, *The Dick Van Dyke Show.* While hosting *Picture This,* he was also the resident comedian on *The Judy Garland Show.* He later starred in *My Mother, the Car.* During the 1978–79 season, he had a co-starring role in *13 Queens Boulevard.*

*Picture This,* although only a three-month summer replacement, made the Nielson Top 10 list for audience popularity. Ben Joelson and Art Baer are currently producing *The Love Boat.*

1963-1964 Season

*Fireball XL-5: XL-5 Model jet. (Courtesy ITC Entertainment.)*

## FIREBALL XL-5

*Saturday, 10:30–11:00 a.m.: NBC*
*Debut: 10/5/63; Cancellation: 9/25/65*
*Producers: Sylvia and Gerry Anderson*
*Supplier: AP Films/ITC Television Corporation*
*Voices: Sylvia Anderson, David Graham, Paul Maxwell, John Bluthal*

This British puppet series was set on 21st-century Earth, in Space City, home of the Galaxy Patrol, a police force of the future. The puppets were animated in "Supermarionation," a technique developed by the show's producers, Sylvia and Gerry Anderson. Supermarionation was a marriage of the traditional marionette with modern solenoid cicuitry. The puppets were made of plastic and equipped with moveable

*Fireball XL-5*: The complete cast. (Courtesy of ITC Entertainment.)

eyeballs and lips. Fine control lines, invisible
to the television viewer, operated the puppets and synchronized their eye and lip
movements to a prerecorded speech tape.

Hero of the Galaxy Patrol was the
square-jawed Colonel Steve Zodiac, pilot of
Fireball XL-5, and a powerful and sophisticated jet fighter. Venus was his female
co-pilot. Additional characters included
Lieutenant 90, a pilot, Professor Metric, the
obligatory science genius, Robert the Robot,
and Commander Zero, the Space City con-
troller. The team brought to justice such villains as Mr. and Mrs. Superspy and the
Briggs Brothers. The latter was an allusion to
racketeer siblings in Britain.

The Andersons continued to perfect
Supermarionation in their series *Stingray*
(1965), the very successful *Thunderbirds*
(1966) and *Joe-90* (1968). ITC Entertainment, producer of television shows and motion pictures, has made a number of science
fiction series, principally for syndication.
These include *Space:1999* and *U.F.O.*

## HECTOR HEATHCOTE

*Saturday, 10:00 – 10:30 a.m.: NBC*
*Debut: 10/5/63; Cancellation: 9/26/64*
*Supplier: Terrytoons*
*Voices: John Myhers*

Hector Heathcote was a well-intentioned
cartoon scientist who invented a means of
traveling backward in time. He used the
technique to relive such historic events as
the French Revolution and the building of
the Pyramids. He never attempted to
change the course of events. He only
wanted to understand the reasons behind
them and to investigate their consequences.
(The producers hired a history professor to
ensure historical accuracy.) In his travels,
Heathcote was always accompanied by his
trusted dog, Winston, who provided moral
support when past events proved to be a
little unpredictable.

Hector shared the program with two

*Hector Heathcote*: Hector Heathcote and a friend. (Courtesy of Viacom International, Inc.)

other cartoon characters: Hashimoto, and Sidney, the Elephant. The former—a Japanese mouse—was a judo expert. The culture, legends and traditions of Japan were amusingly explored through the eyes of Hashimoto and his family. Sidney was a clumsy yet well-meaning 42-year-old pachyderm. His loyal and long-suffering friends, Stanley the lion and Cleo the giraffe, attempted—not always successfully—to prevent Sidney from creating havoc in the African jungle.

The producer of this series was Terrytoons, one of the industry's first and most influential animation studios. Paul Terry and Frank Moser formed the company in 1929, with Bill Weiss joining them in 1930. Eli Bower, a Terrytoons designer, created Hector Heathcote, who had first appeared in a theatrical film titled *The Minute and A Half Man*. The character was seen in a number of movie cartoons before appearing on network television. Terrytoons were also responsible for a number of other cartoon characters, including Heckle and Jeckle, Deputy Dawg, Tom Terrific and Mighty Mouse. Over the years many major independent producers, directors and animators have passed through Terrytoons' portals, including Ralph Bakshi and Lars Bourne.

## THE NEW CASPER CARTOON SHOW

*Saturday, 11:00 – 11:30 a.m.: ABC*
*Debut: 10/5/63; Cancellation: 1/30/70*
*Supplier: Harvey Famous Cartoons*

Casper the friendly ghost was a non-threatening animated apparition. Although he usually frightened people, he continuously sought out human friendships. Casper's supporting cast included Wendy, the Good Witch, Poil, his girl friend, Spooky, the mischievous ghost, and the Ghostly Trio.

Casper was created in 1946 by Joseph

Oriolo, who was then a producer for Paramount Pictures. The cartoons were made by Harvey Famous Cartoons and released to movie theaters by Paramount until the 1950s. Casper came to television in 1953 in a syndicated series of 6½-minute theatrical cartoons. Finally, 10 years later, after gaining a large nationwide following, he was given his own Saturday morning program, *The New Casper Cartoon Show*.

In the late 1970s, Casper returned to television in a Hanna-Barbera series, *Casper and the Space Angels,* which reflected the growing interest in space travel. Casper found himself in the company of a new breed of spectral companions.

The little ghost has been by no means invisible in tie-in merchandise. He is currently a star of comic books, coloring pads, Halloween costumes and other items. He also makes public appearances. His television apparitions are in syndication worldwide.

*The New Casper Cartoon Show*: Casper, Spooky, Wendy the Witch and the Ghostly trio. (Courtesy of Harvey Publications, Inc.)

*New Casper Cartoon Show*: Casper, the friendly ghost. (Courtesy of Harvey Publications, Inc.)

## QUICK DRAW McGRAW

*Saturday, 11:30 – 12:00 noon: CBS*
*Debut: 9/28/63; Cancellation: 9/3/66*
*Supplier: Hanna-Barbera Productions*

*Voices*
*Quick Draw McGraw,*
*Baba Looey, Snooper,*
*Blabber, Augie Doggie,*
*Snagglepuss . . . . . . . . . . . . . . Daws Butler*
*Doggie Daddy . . . . . . . . . . . . Doug Young*

Set in New Mexico, this animated series followed the exploits of Marshal Quick Draw McGraw, a dim-witted horse, who was known as "the slowest gun in the West." He and his assistant, a Mexican burro named Baba Looey, struggled to maintain law and order on the lawless frontier. The duo frequently crossed paths and guns with outlaws and ne'er-do-wells. They triumphed by default rather than by concerted effort.

Additional segments featured Snagglepuss, a trouble-prone lion, Snooper and Blabber, an incompatible cat and mouse, and Augie Doggie, a bright, if impulsive, canine. Augie was usually bailed out of trouble by his doting and long-suffering father, aptly named Doggie Daddy.

## TENNESSEE TUXEDO AND HIS TALES

*Saturday, 9:30–10:00 a.m.: CBS*
*Debut: 9/28/63; Cancellation: 9/3/66*
*Supplier: TOTAL Television and Leonardo Productions Inc.*

*Quickdraw McGraw*: Quickdraw himself. (Courtesy of Hanna-Barbera Productions.)

*Voices:* Don Adams *(Tennessee Tuxedo),* Kenny Delmar, Jackson Beck, Bradley Bolke, Larry Storch, Ben Stone, Allen Swift, Delo Stokes, Norman Rose, Mort Marshall, George S. Irving, Frank Milano

Tennessee Tuxedo was a cartoon penguin with a quick wit, especially when it came to one-liners. He and his friend Chumley, a simple, easy-going walrus, lived at the Megopolis Zoo, where they frequently complained about living conditions. Unfortunately, their suggestions for improvements fell on the unsympathetic ears of the zoo's curator, Stanley Livingstone.

Tennessee and Chumley were joined by their friend Professor Phineas J. Whoopee, who showed them how to solve every-day problems by applying scientific principles.

At the close of each episode, Professor Whoopee solved scientific problems posed in the story. He answered such questions as: What makes electricity travel along a wire? What is time? and, How do you lift an object four times your weight?

Other cartoons seen on this show were *Tooter the Turtle,* and *The King and Odie* [see **King Leonardo and His Short Subjects** (1960/61)] and *Klondike Kat.* The latter was a lively variation on the classic "cat-and-mouse" story. Klondike was a member of the fine and fearsome Klondike Cops, who patrolled the mining country of the Old West. Much of his time was taken up with the antics of a mouse named Savoir Fare (a play on the French words for "know-how") who had a gourmet's taste in food. The efficient and loyal Malamutt dutifully pulled Savoir Fare around on a sled.

---

*Tennessee Tuxedo and His Tales* (clockwise from left): Tennessee, Chumley, Yak, Baldy and Mr. Whoopee, center. (Courtesy of Leonardo-TTV Productions.)

*Tennessee Tuxedo and His Tales:* Klondike Kat; Savoir Fare, the epicurean mouse thief and Malomutt, Klondike's faithful dog. (Courtesy of Leonardo-TTV Productions.)

*Tennessee Tuxedo and His Tales:* Tennessee and friends. (Courtesy of TTV-Leonardo Productions.)

*Tennessee Tuxedo and His Tales:* Tutor Turtle. (Courtesy of TTV-Leonardo Productions.)

# 1964 - 1965 Season

*The Adventures of Jonny Quest* (left to right): Dr. Benton Quest, Jonny, Bandit, Hadji, and Race Bannon. (Courtesy of Hanna-Barbera Productions.)

# THE ADVENTURES OF JONNY QUEST

**Friday,** 7:30–8:00 p.m.: ABC
**Debut:** 9/18/64; **Cancellation:** 9/9/65
  (ABC)
**Return:** 9/9/67; **Cancellation:** 9/5/70
  (CBS)
**Return:** 9/13/70; **Cancellation:** 9/5/71
  (ABC)
**Return:** 9/11/71; **Cancellation:** 9/2/72
  (ABC)

**Return:** 9/8/79; **Cancellation:** 4/12/80
  (NBC)
**Supplier:** Hanna-Barbera Productions

**Voices**
Jonny Quest . . . . . . . . . .Tim Matthieson
Dr. Benton Quest . . . . . .John Stephenson,
                          Don Messick
Race Bannon . . . . . . . . .Mike Road
Hadji . . . . . . . . . . . . . . .Danny Bravo
Bandit . . . . . . . . . . . . . .Don Messick

Playing for only a year on prime time, this animated family adventure series found its niche on the Saturday morning schedule, where it ran for three years.

Dr. Benton Quest, an eminent anthropologist, coursed the globe in search of scientific phenomena. Quest's traveling companions were his bright and articulate adolescent son Jonny and the boy's young friend Hadji, an Asian Indian. For protection they took along a burly bodyguard named Race Bannon. Bannon's duties included instructing the boys in both academic subjects and survival tactics. Jonny's dog Bandit, so-called for his dark, masklike eye markings, scampered along as well. The group's expeditions led them to explore fossils and all manner of natural mysteries—even prehistoric protagonists. They often raced against the clock, as they attempted to outwit self-obsessed scientists and unscrupulous businessmen.

## THE FAMOUS ADVENTURES OF MR. MAGOO

**Saturday,** 8:00–8:30 p.m.: NBC
**Debut:** 9/19/64; **Cancellation:** 8/21/65
**Supplier:** UPA Pictures

**Voices:** Jim Backus (Mr. Quincy Magoo), Marvin Miller, Howard Morris, Paul Frees

Mr. Magoo, an animated caricature of an irascible, near-sighted old man, bore a strong resemblance to the legendary comedian W. C. Fields. In this series, he portrayed numerous fictional and historical characters. Each week, the nearly blind Mr. Magoo played such roles as Long John Silver, Friar Tuck, William Tell, Rip Van Winkle and Ulysses.

Mr. Magoo first appeared in a supporting role in *Ragtime Bear,* an animated theatrical cartoon produced by UPA circa 1949 and distributed by Columbia Pictures the following year. The success of the feature prompted Columbia to request more Magoo

films. Over the years, UPA produced 43 theatrical shorts, two of which have won Academy Awards: *When Magoo Flew* (1954) and *Mr. Magoo's Puddle-Jumper* (1956). Among the animators at UPA who assisted in the development of Mr. Magoo were John Hubley and Stephen Bosustow.

Building on this success, Mr. Magoo moved into television with 130 five-minute cartoons, produced and syndicated by UPA. On December 18, 1962, the loveable eccentric appeared on network television as Scrooge in *Mr. Magoo's Christmas Carol,* a loose interpretation of the Charles Dickens classic. The program led to this NBC weekly series. Mr. Magoo subsequently appeared in a television special on NBC in February 1970 entitled *Uncle Sam Magoo.* In the fall of 1977 he resurfaced in a CBS Saturday morning series titled *What's New, Mister Magoo,* produced by DePatie-Freleng.

The character has been a successful marketing device for the General Electric Company. Mr. Magoo has also been seen in commercials and industrial training films for the National Heart Association, Timex, General Foods, Rheingold Beer, Ideal Toys, Dell Publishing, and Colgate-Palmolive, to name a few.

## HOPPITY HOOPER SHOW

**Saturday,** 12:30–1:00 p.m.: ABC
**Debut:** 9/12/64; **Cancellation:** 9/2/67
**Supplier:** Hooper-Ward Productions

**Voices**
Hoppity Hooper . . . . . . . . . .Chris Allen
Waldo Wigglesworth . . . . . .Hans Conried
Fillmore . . . . . . . . . . . . . . . .Bill Scott
Commander McBragg . . . . .Kenny Delmar
Bullwinkle . . . . . . . . . . . . . .Bill Scott
Rocky . . . . . . . . . . . . . . . . .June Foray
Boris Badenov . . . . . . . . . .Paul Frees

This animated series had a quality reminiscent of Kenneth Grahame's classic children's

The Giant . . . . . . . . . . . .*Jonathan Winters*
Sugar Bear . . . . . . . . . .*Sterling Holloway*

**Other characters:** *Loveable Truly, The Postman, Royal Raccoon, So Hi the Chinese Boy, Billi Bird*

Linus, a cartoon king of the beasts, was a good-natured and kindly lion, leader of the animals in an African jungle. Linus was conceived as a product symbol for General Foods breakfast cereals by Gene Schinto, a copy writer for Benton & Bowles, the New York advertising agency. His partner, Ed Graham, had been a writer, director and producer for the memorable TV commercials of the comedy team of Bob Elliot and Ray Goulding. Sheldon Leonard provided an appropriate voice for the character.

Their Linus commercials were an immediate success, and it was only a short step to an animated series with Linus as the star. Additional characters came off the drawing boards, and Carl Reiner and Jonathan Winters headed a formidable list of famous performers who provided the voices. General Foods saw the advantage of including other product symbols in the series. Consequently, Sugar Bear and The Postman were added to the cast.

This profitable series was doubly important to General Foods, and the company in-

---

*Linus, the Lion-Hearted*: Linus. (Courtesy of Ed Graham Productions.)

sisted on high standards of production. A half-hour segment of the show cost in excess of $87,000, close to three times the norm at that time. *Linus* came to an end in 1969, when the Federal Trade Commission ruled that a character used in a commercial could not appear in a program. The reasoning was that children are not sufficiently discriminatory to be able to separate one from the other.

## MISTER MAYOR

*Saturday, 8:00 – 9:00 a.m.: CBS*
*Debut: 9/26/64; Cancellation: 9/18/65*
*Supplier: Robert Keeshan Associates*
*Cast: Robert Keeshan (Mister Mayor), Jane Connell, Bill McCutcheon, Cosmo Allegretti*
*Puppeteer: Cosmo Allegretti*

The CBS network conceived this program as a replacement for *Captain Kangaroo,* starring Bob Keeshan, then airing six mornings a week. It was developed by Keeshan himself, according to the instructions of network executives, who felt that he needed a more versatile character in a similar format. As in **Captain Kangaroo,** several of his supporting players were puppets. Mister Mayor was a diplomatic community leader who had a talent for communicating with all types of people. He could offer a "shoulder to cry on," or "soothe ruffled feathers" in the event of a dispute. Among those he helped were Aunt Maud, Dudley, Miss Melissa, and the show's comedian, Rollo the Hippopotamus.

    *Mister Mayor* replaced *Captain Kangaroo* for nearly a year before being cancelled in 1965 to allow for the Captain's welcome return.

## THE PORKY PIG SHOW

*Saturday, 10:30 – 11:00 a.m.: ABC*
*Debut: 9/13/64; Cancellation: 9/3/65*
*Supplier: Warner Brothers*
*Voice: Mel Blanc (Porky Pig)*

Looney Tunes' stuttering cartoon pig has been seen in theatrical shorts, on television and in TV cartoon anthologies. He became the host of his own show with this Saturday morning series. Also featured were these animated cartoons: *Daffy Duck, Bugs Bunny, Sylvester and Tweety, Foghorn Leghorn* and *Pepe le Pew.*

    Created by Fritz Freleng in 1934, Porky Pig has been drawn by many animators since then. A mild-mannered and naive little pig, he is usually the butt of others' jokes. Frequently acting on the spur of the moment, he often finds himself being helped out of tight spots by such friends as Daffy Duck and Sylvester the cat. He never seems to learn from his frequently painful experiences. The striking characters ensure a never-ending supply of funny adventures. For example, there is Pepe le Pew, the *bon vivant* of animation. An amorous skunk with a French accent, he once ardently pursued a female cat accidentally adorned with a white stripe. He is known for his melodic crooning of *"Toujours, l'amour, toujours."* (Always, love!)

    *Foghorn Leghorn* is a "Kentucky Fried" rooster with a Southern accent. A cocky bird, he is given to such expressions as "Listen to me, Son!" He often croons his favorite tune, "Camptown Races."

    Although no longer featured in his own show, Porky continues to be seen in CBS-TV's *The Bugs Bunny/Road Runner Show.* This series is comprised of footage from earlier theatrical shorts.

*Porky Pig Show*: The many faces of Porky Pig.
(Courtesy of Warner Communications, Inc.)

*Porky Pig Show*: Porky Pig on the move. (Courtesy of Warner Communications, Inc.)

# SHENANIGANS

*Saturday, 10:00–10:30 a.m.: ABC*
*Debut: 9/26/64, Cancellation: 12/18/65*
*Supplier: Heatter-Quigley Productions*
*Host: Stubby Kaye*
*Announcer: Kenny Williams*

*Shenanigans* was an apt name for this lively game show. The format consisted of a huge game board marked out in squares that covered the studio floor. Two juvenile contestants surmounted obstacles by successfully answering questions or performing tasks, as indicated in the squares. The first contestant to reach "home" received play money that could be exchanged for merchandise.

*Shenanigans* originated locally in 1952 on New York station WPIX. It was initially hosted by Bob Quigley, who was replaced by the rotund Stubby Kaye for the network presentation. The sponsor was Milton Bradley, the toy and game manufacturer.

1965-1966 Season

*Underdog*: The Hunter and the Fox. (Courtesy of Leonardo-TTV Productions.)

## THE ATOM ANT SHOW

**Saturday, 9:30–10:00 a.m.: NBC**
**Debut: 10/2/65; Cancellation: 9/2/67**
**Supplier: Hanna-Barbera Productions**

**Voices**

Atom Ant . . . . . . . . . . . . . .Howard Morris,
                                Don Messick
Precious Pup . . . . . . . . . . .Don Messick
Granny Sweet . . . . . . . . .Janet Waldo
Paw Rugg . . . . . . . . . . . . .Henry Corden
Maw Rugg . . . . . . . . . . . . .Jean VanderPyl
Flora Rugg . . . . . . . . . . . .Jean Vander-Pyl
Shag Rugg . . . . . . . . . . . .Don Messick

This superhero insect was an atomic-powered dot that soared into action against hapless villains. (The nuclear powered aircraft carrier U.S.S. Enterprise recently se-lected Atom Ant as the ship's official mascot.)

*The Atom Ant Show* also featured *The Hillbilly Bears*, a family of brown bears living deep in the hill country of Arkansas, and *Precious Pup*, a sneaky rascal owned by Granny Sweet. Atom Ant was one of the first Hanna-Barbera cartoon characters created especially for Saturday-morning audiences. The series was subsequently incorporated into **The Atom Ant/Secret Squirrel Show** (1967/68).

*The Atom Ant Show*: Atom Ant. (Courtesy of
Hanna-Barbera Productions.)

name from his uncanny ability to bounce off objects, like a bullet, without suffering injury.

Punkin' Puss (a cat) and Mush Mouse are hillbillies trying to survive the travails of mountain country. Since the cancellation of *Magilla Gorilla,* the cartoons have appeared in other Hanna-Barbera compilations.

## MILTON THE MONSTER

*Saturday, 12:30–1:00 p.m.: ABC*
*Debut: 10/9/65; Cancellation: 9/2/67*
*Supplier: Hal Seeger Productions*

*Voices: Bob McFadden, Beverly Arnold*

Milton was a loveable monster straight from the laboratory of Dr. Frankenstein. With a shuffling gait and "Gomer Pyle's personality," he was not quite the horror his architects intended him to be. Professor Weirdo and Count Kook (a parody of Dracula) had injected a bit too much tenderness into their lumbering monster. Consequently, Milton tried to befriend everyone he met.

Also seen in this series were the following cartoons: *Flukey Luke* was a country-raised cowpoke turned big-city detective. His simple approach to crime often created more trouble than he and his accomplice, an Irish-Indian called "Two Feathers," had bargained for. *Muggy Doo* was a wise-cracking, fast-talking, sly fox. *Penny Penguin* was a precocious little girl, who wore a polka-dot bow and an innocent smile. She insisted on offering help where it was neither required nor wanted, causing endless confusion and frustration. *Stuffy Durma,* the heir to a million dollars, preferred to live the life of a hobo, against all advice.

A principal feature in the series was *The Adventures of Fearless Fly.* This mini-hero fought a never-ending, single-handed crusade against the world's evils in a series of nerve-tickling situations. When off-duty, to avoid recognition, Fearless removed his superpowered glasses and became kindly Hyram the Fly. The latter would "never hurt a fly."

The cartoons were produced in New York by Hal Seeger; they were syndicated by Worldvision.

*Milton the Monster*: Milton and his monstrous friends. (Courtesy of Hal Seeger Productions.)

## THE SECRET SQUIRREL SHOW

*Saturday, 10:00–10:30 a.m.: NBC*
*Debut: 10/2/65; Cancellation: 9/2/67*
*Supplier: Hanna-Barbera Productions*

### Voices
Secret Squirrel . . . . . . . . . *Mel Blanc*
Morocco Mole . . . . . . . . . *Paul Frees*
Chief Winchley . . . . . . . . *John Stephenson*
Winsome Witch . . . . . . . . *Paul Frees*

The popularity of Ian Fleming's celebrated spy James Bond, Agent 007, inspired this animated cartoon series. Secret Squirrel, alias Agent 000, wore an overlong trench coat, with the collar turned up, and a hat with a low brim that shaded his eyes. Squirrel sought out villains in such unlikely places as fountain pens and potted plants. The undercover sleuth was equipped with the proper Bond gadgets, from a wristwatch transmitter to a duplicate head, the latter to create confusion as to his whereabouts.

His accomplice was Morocco Mole, a character straight out of a North African bazaar, sporting a tassled fez. Appropriately Morocco had an acute sense of smell, which compensated for his almost total blindness. Both characters were worthy of Fleming. They chased many forms of low life, but the frequent focus of their attentions was a particularly evil character called *Yellow Pinky*—an obvious allusion to the movie *Goldfinger*.

Also on this show was *Squiddly Diddly*, a cartoon featuring a squid who was the janitor of a sea aquarium. Squiddly was determined to become a movie star, and he hoped to be "discovered" while entertaining audiences at the nautical amusement park, where he worked. He invariably overlooked his janitorial responsibilities. A second cartoon feature was *The Winsome Witch*—one of the good kind—who used her black hat, broom and strange powers to assist those in need. This series ran for two years and returned during the 1967/68 season. The likeable squirrel was teamed with a heroic insect in ***The Atom Ant/Secret Squirrel Show*** (1967/68).

*The Secret Squirrel Show:* Secret Squirrel,
Squiddly Diddly and his friend Chief Winchly.
(Courtesy of Hanna-Barbera Productions.)

*Tom and Jerry: The* cat and mouse. (Courtesy of MGM, Copyright 1940 Loew's Inc.; Copyright renewed by MGM, Inc.)

## TOM AND JERRY

*Saturday, 11:00 – 11:30 a.m.: CBS*
*Debut: 9/25/65; Cancellation: 9/17/72*
*Supplier: Hanna-Barbera Productions*

*Vocal effects: Mel Blanc, June Foray*

The inimitable Tom and Jerry, the warring cat and mouse, were the focus of this animated series. It was based on the famous MGM theatrical shorts, which won seven Oscars.

*Tom and Jerry* was created by Joseph Barbera and William Hanna, the namesakes of Hanna-Barbera Productions, while they were under contract to MGM studios in the 1940s. A number of other well-known cartoon directors contributed to the film series over the years, including Chuck Jones (Warner Brothers), Gene Deitch (Terrytoons), Ben Washam, Abe Levitow, Tom Ray and Jim Pabian. The critical acclaim showered on the shorts led CBS to purchase rights to the characters for a Hanna-Barbera Saturday morning cartoon. The TV version of *Tom and Jerry* was made to appeal to a significantly younger home audience.

During the 1940s and 1950s, when the cartoons were produced for the big screen, the budget was considerably larger than the subsequent television production. This smaller budget imposed technical restrictions. Trimming the animation expenditure, Barbera and Hanna created a new technique called "limited animation." Usually there are sixteen drawings required for one linear foot of full animation. In limited animation, that number can be reduced to five and one-half per linear foot, resulting in considerable production savings.

*Tom and Jerry* ran on CBS for seven years. After cancellation in 1972, it resurfaced in 1975 in a new cartoon, *The Tom and Jerry/Grape Ape Show.*

## ANIMAL SECRETS

*Saturday, 1:00 – 1:30 p.m.: NBC*
*Debut: 10/15/66; Cancellation: 4/8/67*
*Supplier: The Graphic Curriculum, in as-*
*    sociation with Public Affairs Dept., NBC*
*Narrator/Host: Dr. Loren Eiseley*

Dr. Loren Eiseley, a renowned anthropologist at the University of Pennsylvania, hosted
this documentary series. The subject was the
animal kingdom. Hibernation, seasonal
changes, migratory habits and other aspects
of animal life were explored, using stock
wildlife footage.

Each episode concentrated on a specific
natural mystery, such as: What makes a bee
buzz? How do fish communicate? Originally
programmed by NBC on Saturdays, *Animal
Secrets* also aired on prime time in July and
August of 1967.

## THE BEAGLES

*Saturday, 12:30 – 1:00 p.m.: CBS*
*Debut: 9/10/66; Cancellation: 9/2/67*
*    (CBS)*
*Return: 9/9/67; Cancellation: 9/7/68*
*    (ABC)*
*Supplier: TOTAL Television*

*The Beagles* were a canine rock & roll duo
named Stringer and Tubby. The pups
crooned their way through various adventures. Produced by the creators of **Underdog** (1964/65) and **Tennessee Tuxedo**
(1963/64), the show was a parody of the
Beatles. The Liverpudlian rock group was
enjoying tremendous popularity at the time.

## COOL McCOOL

*Saturday, 11:00 – 11:30 a.m.: NBC*
*Debut: 9/10/66; Cancellation: 8/31/68*
*Return: 5/17/69; Cancellation: 8/30/69*
*Supplier: King Features Syndicate*

*King Kong*: Tom of T.H.U.M.B. (Courtesy of Rankin/Bass Productions.)

*The Lone Ranger*: The Lone Ranger and Silver. (Courtesy of the Wrather Corporation.)

*The Lone Ranger*: The Lone Ranger and trusted companion, Tonto. (Courtesy of the Wrather Corporation.)

# THE NEW ADVENTURES OF SUPERMAN

*Saturday, 11:00 – 11:30 a.m.: CBS*
*Debut: 9/10/66; Cancellation: 9/2/67*
*Supplier: Filmation Associates*

## Voices

Clark Kent/Superman . . . .Bud Collyer
Lois Lane . . . . . . . . . . . . .Joan Alexander
**Narrator:** *Jackson Beck*

This was television's first animated cartoon version of America's oldest and best-loved superhero.

Superman was created in 1938 by Joe Schuster and Jerry Siegel for Action Comics (published by DC Comics, then owned by National Periodical Publications). Superman quickly gathered a substantial and loyal following, appearing in a series of theatrical cartoons and movie serials. In 1953 George Reeves starred in a syndicated TV series that is still being shown locally across the country. Its enduring success led to this network Saturday morning show.

As in the comic book, episodes followed the adventures of Clark Kent (alias Superman), a reporter for *The Daily Planet*. His colleague, Lois Lane, harbored doubts about Clark's identity and irregular behavior. There was an unspoken attachment between the two, which fueled the young woman's inquisitiveness. Clark tried to conceal his alter ego by giving the impression of being fragile and overly cautious. Although occasionally given to comedy, the series remained dramatic and generally faithful to the comic book legend.

Also featured were the animated exploits of *Superboy*—the Caped Crusader as a teenager. This segment was set in his home town, where he lived with his adoptive parents and his pet superdog, Krypto.

*The New Adventures of Superman* remained on CBS for a full year. The following season, the Man of Steel was paired with *Aquaman*, also a joint venture of DC Comics and Filmation Associates, in **The**

*Superman-Aquaman Hour of Adventure* (1967/68). The subsequent season saw a further change with Superman co-starring with the Caped Crusader in *The Batman-Superman Hour* (1968/69). He returned to Saturday mornings during the 1973/74 season on ABC as a character in Hanna-Barbera's cartoon series, *The Superfriends*.

Jerry Siegel and Joe Schuster, who had signed away the rights to the Superman phenomenon, received no royalties for their efforts, until the release of the box-office hit movie in 1978. The copyright had been secured in the name of DC Comics. The pair filed suit, and Warner Communications, which now owned DC, agreed to a modest annual p   .on for each of $20,000 for the rest o'  .eir lives.

# THE ROAD RUNNER

*Saturday, 12:00 – 12:30 p.m.: CBS*
*Debut: 9/10/66; Cancellation: 9/7/68*
*Supplier: Warner Brothers*

*Voices: Mel Blanc*

This animated series was comprised of old theatrical shorts and new TV cartoons. It featured one of Warner Brothers' oldest and most popular cartoon characters, the Road Runner.

The fleet-footed bird was always a step or more ahead of his determined pursuer, Wile E. Coyote, who was destined never to have Road Runner as dinner. Wile E. Coyote was a desert scavenger who constantly attempted to trap the fast-moving bird. Being incorrigibly cheap, the coyote frequently used discount devices from the "ACME" warehouse to bring home the meal he craved. At every turn his efforts were botched either by ACME defects or by the Road Runner himself. The bird would always speed away with a wry smile on his beak and a triumphal "Beep! Beep!"

*The Road Runner Show*: The Road Runner beeping along. (Courtesy of Warner Communications, Inc.)

The show subsequently became a segment of CBS's ***The Bugs Bunny/Road Runner Hour*** (1968/69). In 1971 the program switched to ABC and ran on Saturdays until 1972, under the title *The Road Runner Show*. In 1972 it became part of *The Bugs Bunny/Road Runner Show* on CBS.

*The Road Runner Show*: The Star of the show and Wile E. Coyote (Courtesy of Warner Communications, Inc.)

1980

1980

1966

1980

*Space Ghost and Dino Boy*: Space Ghost and Dino Boy. (Courtesy of Hanna-Barbera Productions.)

## SPACE GHOST AND DINO BOY

**Saturday,** *10:30 – 11:00 a.m.: CBS*
**Debut:** *9/10/66;* **Cancellation:** *9/7/68*
**Supplier:** *Hanna-Barbera Productions*

### Voices

Space Ghost . . . . . . . . . . . *Gary Owens*
Jan . . . . . . . . . . . . . . . . . . . . *Jinny Tyler*
Jayce . . . . . . . . . . . . . . . . . *Tim Matthieson*
Dino Boy . . . . . . . . . . . . . *Johnny Carson*
Ugh . . . . . . . . . . . . . . . . . . *Mike Road*

This animated series fitted in well with the prevailing Saturday morning riptide of superheroes who performed incredible deeds.

Space Ghost, wearing a black and white costume, was an interplanetary crime-fighter. He was assisted by his two teenage wards, Jan and Jayce, and their pet space monkey, Blip. The ethereal crusader wore a magic belt that gave him the ability to fly and to become invisible. He possessed great strength and had the ability to fire energy beams from his fingertips. His companions shared none of Space Ghost's superpowers, although they were able to fly—courtesy of their magic belts.

The supporting segment, *Dino Boy*, followed the adventures of a young man named Tod, and Ugh, the caveman. Tod's father had been killed in a time-warp accident that left his son in prehistoric times. Ugh saved the boy from a hungry saber-toothed tiger, and the pair become inseparable friends.

*Space Ghost* has resurfaced from time to

time; it was rerun on NBC during the 1970s. The character returned in NBC's all-new *Space Stars* during the 1981/82 season.

## THE SPACE KIDETTES

*Saturday, 10:30–11:00 a.m.: NBC*
*Debut: 9/10/66; Cancellation: 9/2/67*
*Supplier: Hanna-Barbera Productions*

#### Voices

Scooter . . . . . . . . . . . . . . . . . . .*Chris Allen*
Snoopy . . . . . . . . . . . . . . . . . .*Lucille Bliss*
Countdown . . . . . . . . . . . . . .*Don Messick*
Jenny . . . . . . . . . . . . . . . . . .*Janet Waldo*
Pupstar . . . . . . . . . . . . . . . . .*Don Messick*
Captain Skyhook . . . . . . . . . .*Daws Butler*
Static . . . . . . . . . . . . . . . . . . .*Daws Butler*

In a season bursting with superheroes, this series featured a futuristic group of young crime-fighters in the "Our Gang" mold. The team consisted of Scooter, Snoopy (not to be confused with the beagle in Charles Schultz's comic strip, *Peanuts*), Countdown, Jenny, and Pupstar, their dog.

The Space Kidettes were outfitted in space uniforms and helmets. They lived in their rocket "clubhouse," roaming the galaxies. When moving around outside the rocket, they wore jet-packs fastened to their backs. Their main antagonist was Captain Skyhook—a parody of Captain Hook in *Peter Pan*—and his incompetent associate Static. The cantankerous British captain often vented his frustrations on Static when his plans went awry. Static was half the captain's height, and the two maintained a relationship similar to that of Laurel and Hardy. Skyhook's bark was invariably worse than his bite. Often the Kidettes, Skyhook and Static would rescue each other when a villainous third party, a space dragon, for example, intervened. "Boil them in Moon oil!" was Skyhook's favorite threat to his young rivals, although he never followed through with it.

*Space Kidettes*: Captain Skyhook and the kidettes. (Courtesy of Hanna-Barbera Productions.)

# THE SUPER SIX

*Saturday, 9:00 – 9:30 a.m.: NBC*
**Debut:** *9/10/66;* **Cancellation:** *9/6/69*
**Supplier:** *DePatie - Freleng / Mirisch - Rich Productions in conjunction with United Artists*

### Voices

Super Bwoing ...........*Charles Smith*
The Brothers Matzoriley ...*Paul Frees and*
*Daws Butler*
Captain Wammy .........*Paul Frees*
Magnet Man .............*Daws Butler*
Elevator Man ...........*Paul Stewart*
Super Scuba ...........*Arte Johnson*
Granite Man ............*Lyn Johnson*

This animated series featured the adventures of "Super Service Inc.," a superhero team available for hire. The team was made up of Granite Man, Super Scuba, Elevator Man, Magnet Man, and Captain Wammy, all of whose names coincided with their superpowers. An additional weekly segment featured Super Bwoing, a guitar strumming daredevil, and the Irish-Jewish brothers Matzoriley.

This was DePatie-Freleng's first TV production since their highly successful *Pink Panther* shorts.

*The Fantastic Four*: The Thing and the Human Torch. (Copyright 1981 Marvel Comics Group, a division of Cadence Industries Corp.)

Reed Richards, a brilliant scientist affectionately known as Mr. Fantastic, had the ability to lengthen his body and perform acrobatic feats. His wife Sue, otherwise known as the Invisible Girl, had the power to make herself or her enemies invisible. She could also project an invisible force-field as a means of defense. Johnny Storm, Sue's younger brother, was called the Human Torch. He had the ability to "flame on" a devastating, heat-generating power. Ben Grimm, The Thing, was transformed into a living rock with the strength of a thousand men. Episodes followed the group's worldwide rescue adventures.

Stan Lee, of Marvel Comics, originated the fearsome four in 1961. He is also responsible for Spider-Man, Dr. Strange and other highly regarded superhero comic-book characters seen on television. He has become a legend in the comic-book industry for his originality and writing skills.

In the late 1970s, a new *Fantastic Four* series appeared on NBC on Saturday mornings. It was produced by DePatie-Freleng.

*The Fantastic Four*: The series' heroes. (Copyright 1981 Marvel Comics Group, A division of Cadence Industries Corp.)

MISTER FANTASTIC™

INVISIBLE GIRL™

*George of the Jungle*: George, Shep the elephant  and Ursala the native girl. (Courtesy of P.A.T./ Ward Productions.)

## GEORGE OF THE JUNGLE

**Saturday,** *11:30 – 12:00 noon: ABC*
**Debut:** *9/9/67; **Cancellation:** 9/15/70*
**Supplier:** *Jay Ward Productions*

**Voices:** *Bill Scott, June Foray, Paul Frees, Bill Conrad, Walter Tetley, Skip Craig, Barbara Baldwin*

This animated spoof of Tarzan featured a clumsy, tree-swinging jungle lord named George. With an inane grin on his face and a wild, echoing cry, he swung to the rescue of animals and fair maidens in distress, always landing flat on his face. This was usually a result of his meeting a tree en route.

George lived in the Imgwee Gwee Valley in Africa, where he was frequently harassed by the jungle's infamous friends, Tiger and Weavel. George's allies were Bella and Ursula—two native girls—Ape, his pet gorilla, Shep, the elephant, and Seymour and Wiggy, a man-eating plant and a rhinoceros.

The program had two support cartoon

*George of the Jungle*: George doing what he does best. (Courtesy of P.A.T./Ward Productions.)

features, *Super Chicken* and *Tom Slick*. Super Chicken, aptly christened "Henry Cabot Henhouse III," was a mild-mannered scientist. Among his experimental discoveries was "Super-Sauce," a liquid that transformed him into a dauntless, superheroic crime-fighter. His friend and associate, Fred the rooster, assisted him, whenever possible. Tom Slick, a rather stupid race-car driver, tried to put his fast driving to good use, with a little help from his accomplice, Marigold. Tom's car was called the Thunderbolt Grease Slapper; it was one of the fastest things on four wheels.

Jay Ward and Bill Scott, producers of the series, created such memorable cartoon characters as Rocky the flying squirrel, Bullwinkle the moose, and Dudley Do-Right of the Mounties. Although cancelled in 1970, *George of the Jungle* continues to appear in syndication.

## HAPPENING '68

*Saturday, 1:30–2:00 p.m.: ABC*
*Debut: 1/6/68; Cancellation: 9/20/69*
*Supplier: Dick Clark Productions*
*Hosts: Paul Revere, Mark Lindsay*
*Regulars: Freddie Welles, Keith Allison, The Raiders*

This trendy musical variety series was hosted by Paul Revere and Mark Lindsay, with musical accompaniment from Paul's rock band, "The Raiders."

The show featured guest appearances by popular musicians and singers, and up-and-coming performers. Teenagers gave news reports from around the country, and short films produced by high school and college students were shown. There were also comedy sketches and fashion shows. Each week, amateur bands competed in a talent contest. The program asked the rhetorical question, "What's happening in TV land?"

*Happening '68*: Paul Revere and the Raiders in front of a studio audience. (Courtesy of Dick Clark Productions.)

*The Herculoids*: The major characters. (Courtesy of Hanna-Barbera Productions.)

The reply was always, "Happening '68." Dick Clark, the series' producer, had taken his show *American Bandstand* from a local Philadelphia show to an unprecedented run on the ABC network. He subsequently became a major force in the entertainment industry.

## THE HERCULOIDS

**Saturday, 9:30 – 10:00 a.m.: CBS**
**Debut:** *9/9/67;* **Cancellation:** *9/6/69*
**Supplier:** *Hanna-Barbera Productions*

**Voices**
Zandor .................Mike Road
Tarra ...................Virginia Gregg
Zok .....................Mike Road
Domo...................Teddy Eccles
Gloop ..................Don Messick
Gleep ..................Don Messick
Igoo ....................Mike Road

This animated series took place in an idyllic future world, which was from time to time threatened by creatures from other galaxies. Its monarch, King Zandor, engaged a group of bizarre and powerful animal custodians, called the Herculoids, to defend the kingdom. Tarra was Zandor's wife. The Herculoids consisted of: Zok, a dragon who breathed laser beams rather than fire; Dorno, a ten-legged rhinoceros who pelted intruders with pellets from his horn-shaped trunk, Gloop and Gleep, amorphous blobs with the ability to assume the shapes of crushing weapons; and Igoo, a living, gorilla-shaped rock with tremendous strength.

*The Herculoids* has been widely syndicated. The characters were recently updated for NBC's *Space Stars,* also a Hanna-Barbera Production.

## JOURNEY TO THE CENTER OF THE EARTH

*Saturday, 10:30 – 11:00 a.m.: CBS*
*Debut: 9/9/67; Cancellation: 8/30/69*
*Supplier: Filmation Associates*

### Voices
Oliver Lindenbrook . . . . . . . *Ted Knight*
Alec Hewit . . . . . . . . . . . . . *Pat Harrington*
Cindy Lindenbrook . . . . . . . *Jane Webb*
Lars . . . . . . . . . . . . . . . . . . *Pat Harrington*
Count Saccnuson . . . . . . . . *Ted Knight*
Torg . . . . . . . . . . . . . . . . . . *Pat Harrington*

Based on the Jules Verne classic, this Saturday morning cartoon concerned an archaeological team that attempted to return to the Earth's surface while trapped deep within its core.

The program's hero was Professor Oliver Lindenbrook, who discovered the long-lost trail of Arnie Saccnuson, a lone explorer who had died while attempting to penetrate the Earth's center. After organizing an expedition to achieve what his predecessor had begun, Lindenbrook began the long and arduous journey. Accompanying him were his niece Cindy, Alec Hewit, a student, Lars, their guide, and Lindenbrook's pet duck, Gertrude. The team was unaware that the evil Count Saccnuson (the last living relative of the dead explorer) was following them. Saccnuson was determined to claim the Earth's core for his own sinister purposes, and, to this end, he instructed his servant Torg to dynamite the cavern entrance of the core. The blast managed to block the expedition's retreat, as well as Saccnuson's, trapping them all deep inside the Earth.

Ted Knight, the voice of Lindenbrook, has been heard in a number of Saturday morning cartoons. He secured a strong following as the raucous newsman Ted Baxter on the prime-time situation comedy, *The Mary Tyler Moore Show.* He currently stars in his own ABC situation comedy, *Too Close For Comfort.* Pat Harrington (Alec Hewit), is best known for his portrayal of Schneider in the CBS sitcom *One Day at a Time.*

## MOBY DICK AND THE MIGHTY MIGHTOR

*Saturday, 11:00 – 11:30 a.m.: CBS*
*Debut: 9/9/67; Cancellation: 9/6/69*
*Supplier: Hanna-Barbera Productions*

### Voices
Tom . . . . . . . . . . . . . . . . *Bobby Resnick*
Tub . . . . . . . . . . . . . . . . . *Barry Balkin*
Scooby, the seal . . . . . . . *Don Messick*
Mightor . . . . . . . . . . . . . . *Paul Stewart*
Tor . . . . . . . . . . . . . . . . . *Bobby Diamond*
Sheera . . . . . . . . . . . . . . *Patsy Garrett*
Pondo . . . . . . . . . . . . . . . *John Stephenson*
L'il Rock . . . . . . . . . . . . . *Norma McMillan*
Ork . . . . . . . . . . . . . . . . . *John Stephenson*
Tog . . . . . . . . . . . . . . . . . *John Stephenson*

Loosely based on the Herman Melville classic, this animated cartoon characterized the legendary white whale as a hero rather than as an agent of destruction. Tom and Tub, two shipwrecked youngsters, were saved by Moby, who used his immense size and power to protect them and their pet seal, Scooby. Episodes depicted their adventures together as they roamed the seas.

*The Mighty Mightor* shared the half-hour spot with *Moby Dick.* The title character of the cartoon was a prehistoric teenager with secret powers. These enabled him to transform himself from a meek youth to an all-powerful superhero, in the style of Billy Batson/Captain Marvel. Mightor flew to the aid of those in distress, armed with a caveman's club, the only outward sign of his origins.

*Moby Dick and the Mighty Mightor*: Moby Dick, Tom, Tub and Scooby the seal. (Courtesy of Hanna-Barbera Productions.)

## OFF TO SEE THE WIZARD

*Friday, 7:30 – 8:30 p.m.: ABC*
*Debut: 9/8/67; Cancellation: 9/20/68*
*Executive Producer: Chuck Jones in association with MGM*
*Producer/Director: Abe Levitow*

The hosts of this animated cartoon series were characters from *The Wizard of Oz*, including Dorothy, the Cowardly Lion and Toto. They introduced theatrical movies such as *The Adventures of Huckleberry Finn*, *Flipper* and *Clarence the Cross-Eyed Lion*. The films were presented in two episodes, shown on consecutive weeks. These were interspersed with made-for-television material, including nature documentaries and "Who's Afraid of Mother Goose?" This was a live-action interpretation of the Mother Goose stories. Episodes included

"Jack and Jill," starring Frankie Avalon and Nancy Sinatra in the title roles, and Dan Rowan and Steve Martin as, respectively, Simple Simon and the Pieman.

## SAMSON AND GOLIATH

*Saturday, 10:30 – 11:00 a.m.: NBC*
*Debut: 9/9/67; Cancellation: 9/7/68*
*Supplier: Hanna-Barbera Productions*

*Voices: Tim Matthieson (Samson)*

This adventure series concerned the activities of a boy named Samson and his dog Goliath. Both were clandestine superheroes. Whenever the need arose, Samson would close one wrist over the other, and invoke the words "I need Samson Power!" Instantaneously, the boy was transformed into that pillar of biblical strength, Samson, and his dog into a powerful lion. Together, they battled a variety of evil characters. They always won out in the end.

Segments of this show were sometimes devoted to the adventures of the Space Kidettes [See also: **The Space Kidettes** (1966/67)].

## SHAZZAN!

*Saturday, 10:00–10:30 a.m.: CBS*
*Debut: 9/9/67; Cancellation: 9/6/69*
*Supplier: Hanna-Barbera Productions*

*Voices*
Shazzan . . . . . . . . . . . . . . . .Barney Phillips
Nancy . . . . . . . . . . . . . . . .Janet Walde
Chuck . . . . . . . . . . . . . . . .Jerry Dexter

Twins Nancy and Chuck found two halves of a ring and joined them together. The restored ring transported the children back through time to the land of the Arabian Knights. The magic ring also provided them with a protector, the 60-foot tall and all-powerful genie "Shazzan." He assisted the children each week in their attempts to return to the present. The journeys frequently exposed them to dangers, as well as the colorful peoples, of bygone eras.

## SPIDER-MAN

*Saturday, 10:00–10:30 a.m.: ABC*
*Debut: 9/9/67; Cancellation: 8/30/69*
*Return: 3/22/70; Cancellation: 9/6/70*
*Supplier: Krantz Films and Grant/Ray/ Lawrence*

*Samson and Goliath*: The powerful duo. (Courtesy of Hanna-Barbera.)

*Shazzan*: Shazzan, Chuck, Nancy, and their flying camel Kbaoobie. (Courtesy of Hanna-Barbera.)

## Voices

Peter Parker/
  Spider-Man . . . . . . . . . .*Bernard Cowen,*
                        *Paul Sols*
Betty Brandt . . . . . . . . . . .*Peg Dixon*
J. Jonah Jameson . . . . . .*Paul Kligman*

Based on the popular Marvel Comics comic-book character, *Spider-Man* featured a maladroit superhero, who was, in reality, a college student and freelance photographer named Peter Parker. While visiting a science exhibition, Parker was accidentally bitten by a spider which had been exposed to nuclear radiation. Its sting imparted certain bizarre powers to the hero, which he used to combat injustice. Parker had the ability to crawl up walls and swing on a web shot from his fingertips. He possessed the proportionate strength of a spider, in addition to a highly developed sixth sense for danger.

Being scientifically inclined, Parker created ancillary equipment for escape and capture techniques. Between his academic studies and photographic assignments for *The Daily Bugle,* Parker battled criminals as the costumed and masked Spider-Man. He confronted just about every type of villain, some drawn from old comic books, others created by the series' writers. The supporting characters were Betty Brandt, a stenographer for the newspaper and Peter's companion, and J. Jonah Jameson, the paper's editor. Jameson incessantly chewed on a cigar and invariably spoke unpleasantly to the clumsy Parker/Spider-Man.

*Spider-Man*: Spider-Man in action. (Copyright 1981 Marvel Comics Group, a division of Cadence Industries Corp.)

*Spider-Man*: Spider-Man in action. (Copyright 1981 Marvel Comics Group, a division of Cadence Industries Corp.)

Created by Stan Lee, the character has appeared both in comic books and as a syndicated newspaper strip. What made this cartoon series so unusual was the personal all-too-human life of this superhero, who was given to colds and sneezing attacks at critical moments.

Spider-Man resurfaced in the late 1970s as a prime-time, live-action CBS series produced by Charles Fries. He returned as a Saturday morning cartoon character in the fall of 1981. Entitled *Spider-Man and His Amazing Friends,* the program was produced by Marvel and aired on NBC. Marvel Comics had by this time established its own company to produce TV shows and movies based upon its copyrighted characters. Three animators—Grant Simmons, Ray Patterson, and Robert Lawrence—pooled their talents to produce this original series. Their other productions include *Thor, Sub-Mariner, The Hulk, Iron Man,* and *Captain America.* The team has since disbanded.

## THE SUPERMAN-AQUAMAN HOUR OF ADVENTURE

*Saturday, 11:30 – 12:30 p.m.: CBS*
*Debut: 9/9/67; Cancellation: 9/7/68*
*Supplier: Filmation Associates*

This animated cartoon brought together two of D.C. Comics' most popular characters for an hour of action and heroics. One hero operated above the water line, the other below. Unlike Superman, who hailed from the planet Krypton, Aquaman was the son of a human father and a mermaid.

Other comic book superheroes from the D.C. stable soared in and out of the cartoon episodes. These included the Flash, the Atom, Green Lantern, Hawkman, the Teen Titans, and members of the Justice League. After cancellation of the series, the Superman episodes returned to Saturday mornings in ***The Batman/Superman Hour*** (1968/69).

## SUPER PRESIDENT

*Saturday, 9:30 – 10:00 a.m.: NBC*
*Debut: 9/16/67; Cancellation: 9/14/68*
*Supplier: DePatie-Freleng Enterprises*

*Voices*
James Norcross . . . . . . . . . . . .*Paul Frees*
Richard Vance . . . . . . . . . . . . .*Daws Butler*

James Norcross, the President of the United States, possessed a number of unique powers, which he had acquired as the result of a cosmic storm. Leaping into action as Super President, he fought the most cunning of Washington D.C.'s criminals. He was on a never-ending mission for justice and the "American Way."

*The Spy Shadow* was the program's second cartoon feature. It followed the adventures of Richard Vance, a private detective who operated independently of himself by way of his own shadow. His "two characters" both fought crime, but were often at odds with each other.

# 1968 - 1969 Season

*The Adventures of Gulliver*: Gary Gulliver, his dog Tag and Captain Leech. (Courtesy of Hanna-Barbera.)

## THE ADVENTURES OF GULLIVER

**Saturday, 9:30 – 10:00 a.m.: ABC**
**Debut: 9/14/68; Cancellation: 9/5/70**
**Supplier: Hanna-Barbera Productions**

**Voices:** Jerry Dexter, Allan Melvin, Don Messick, John Stephenson, Ginny Tyler, Herb Vigran

This animated cartoon dispensed with the satire of Jonathan Swift's classic novel, *Gulliver's Travels,* and concentrated instead on fantastic adventure.

Gary Gulliver and his dog Bib set out to find Gary's father; in the process, they are caught in a tropical storm and shipwrecked on the island of Lilliput. Initially, Gulliver and the Lilliputians are suspicious of each other because of their tremendous size difference. However, after confronting and defeating the Lilliputians' feared enemy, Gulliver wins his captors' trust. As allies, they combatted the villainous Captain Leech, who hankered after Gulliver's treasure map.

## THE ARCHIE SHOW

**Saturday, 10:00 – 10:30 a.m.: CBS**
**Debut: 9/14/68; Cancellation: 9/9/69**
**Supplier: Filmation Associates in association with Archie Comics**

**Voices**
Archie Andrews . . . . . . . .Dallas McKennon
Jughead Jones . . . . . . . .Howard Morris
Betty Cooper . . . . . . . . . .Jane Webb
Veronica Lodge . . . . . . . .Jane Webb

*Reggie Mantle* ........*John Erwin*
*Sabrina, the Teenage*
  *Witch* .............*Jane Webb*

Archie is a caricature of the American teen-ager of the 1940s. He was created as a comic-strip character by Bob Montana and John Goldwater. After nearly 30 years on the newsstands, Norm Prescott and Lou Scheimer of Filmation brought the freckle-faced Archie and his adolescent friends to Saturday morning television in this series.

The program offered two 10-minute sketches and a "dance of the week" selec-tion featuring a new song or musical num-ber. Archie and his friends—Jughead Jones, Betty Cooper, Veronica Lodge and Reggie Mantle—were all students at Riverdale High. They formed a rock band, which provided music for the show. The cross-merchandising worked well, and three hit songs materialized: "Sugar, Sugar," "Jingle, Jangle" and "Who's My Baby."

Unlike the heroes who dominated TV screens at this time, these were very current characters audiences could closely identify with.

The show ran in this format for a year, with small changes in its structure. Most of the characters have appeared on the Satur-day schedule for close to 10 years in a variety of shows. The kids continue to frequent the pages of a number of comic books, and they have not gotten a day older. The various TV series are seen in syndication.

## THE BANANA SPLITS ADVENTURE HOUR

*Saturday, 10:30 – 11:30 a.m.: NBC*
***Debut:** 9/7/68;* ***Cancellation:*** *9/5/70*
***Supplier:** Hanna-Barbera Productions*

*Voices*
***The Banana Splits***
*Fleegle* .............*Paul Winchell*

*The Archie Show*: The Archies, playing up a storm. (Courtesy of Archie Comics Publications, Inc.)

Reggie

Veronica

MOOSE 'N' MIDGE

Archie

Bingo . . . . . . . . . . . . .*Daws Butler*
Drooper . . . . . . . . . . .*Allan Melvin*
Snorky . . . . . . . . . . . .*Don Messick*
**The Three Musketeers**
D'Artagnan . . . . . . . . .*Bruce Watson*
Porthos . . . . . . . . . . .*Barney Phillips*
Aramis . . . . . . . . . . . .*Don Messick*
Athos . . . . . . . . . . . . .*Jonathan Harris*
Tooly . . . . . . . . . . . . .*Teddy Eccles*
The Queen . . . . . . . .*Julie Bennett*
Constance . . . . . . . . .*Julie Bennett*
**The Arabian Knights**
Bez . . . . . . . . . . . . . . .*Henry Corden*
Evil Vangore . . . . . . . .*Paul Frees*
Raseem . . . . . . . . . . .*Frank Gerstle*
Princess Nidor . . . . . .*Shari Lewis*
Turban . . . . . . . . . . .*Jay North*
Fariik . . . . . . . . . . . . .*John Stephenson*
**The Hill-Billy Bears**
Paw Rugg . . . . . . . . . .*Henry Corden*
Maw Rugg . . . . . . . .*Jean VanderPyl*
Flora Rugg . . . . . . . .*Jean VanderPyl*
Shagg Rugg . . . . . . . .*Don Messick*
**Danger Island**
Professor Irwin
  Hayden . . . . . . . . . .*Frank Aletter*
Leslie Hayden,
  his daughter . . . . . .*Ronnie Troup*
Link Simmons,
  his assistant . . . . . . .*Jan-Michael Vincent*
Morgan,
  the castaway . . . . . .*Rockie Tarkington*
Chongo . . . . . . . . . . .*Kahana*
Mu-Tan . . . . . . . . . . .*Victory Eberg*
Chu . . . . . . . . . . . . . .*Rodrigo Arrendondo*
**The Micro Adventure**
Professor Carter . . . . .*Don Messick*
Jill Carter . . . . . . . . .*Patsy Garret*
Mike Carter . . . . . . . .*Tommy Cook*

Fleegle, the dog, Drooper, the lion, Bingo, the gorilla, and Snorky, the baby elephant, were all portrayed by actors wearing oversized cloth costumes. They danced, sang and performed comic sketches. This format was later used in the poular shows, *Scat Cat, The Skateboards* and Jim Henson's *Sesame Street*.

Acting as hosts for this hour-long show, the animals introduced cartoons and live-action films. The cartoons included: *The Three Musketeers, The Arabian Knights,* and *The Hill-Billy Bears.* They also introduced two filmed segments: *Danger Island* concerned the adventures of explorer Professor Irwin Hayden and his daughter, and *The Micro Adventure* followed the odyssey of Professor Carter and his children as they explored the suspenseful world of microscopic creatures.

# THE BATMAN/SUPERMAN HOUR

*Saturday, 10:30–11:30 a.m.: CBS*
*Debut: 9/14/68; Cancellation: 9/6/69*
*Supplier: Filmation Associates*

Superman and Batman, the best-known of the comic-book heroes, played in separate segments of this animated feature, based on characters created for D.C. Comics. Superman was no stranger to Saturday morning television, having been previously featured in **The New Adventures of Superman** (1966/67), and **The Superman/Aquaman Hour of Adventure** (1967/68). Batman came to the Saturday schedule after success in comic books, theatrical serials, and his own live-action, prime-time television series, *Batman,* produced by William Dozier.

In this version the Caped Crusader fought all manner of colorful supervillains with Robin, the Boy Wonder. Unlike Superman, Batman had no superpowers. He relied solely on physical fitness and brain power. Batman, alias Bruce Wayne, was a millionaire who lived in "Gotham City." When he was a boy, a robber shot and killed his parents. Swearing revenge on all criminals, he began to train himself as a human fighting machine. He was equipped with all manner of weaponry, some kept in his utility belt, including a "bat-a-rang" (a bat-shaped

boomerang), and gas pellets. His modes of transport included the famous "Batmobile" and the roof-to-roof "Batline." Robin, alias Dick Grayson, was Batman's teenage ward.

Batman resurfaced in his own Saturday morning cartoon, entitled *The New Adventures of Batman*, during the 1976/77 season.

Batman and Superman also appeared together in Hanna-Barbera's *The Superfriends* (1973/74).

## THE BUGS BUNNY/ROAD RUNNER HOUR

*Saturday, 8:30 – 9:30 a.m.: CBS*
*Debut: 9/14/68; Still Running*
*Supplier: Warner Brothers*
*Voices: Mel Blanc*

This is the longest-running cartoon series in the history of Saturday morning television, and it continues to flourish. Both *Bugs*

*The Banana Splits* (left to right): Bingo, Drooper, Snorky and Fleegle. (Courtesy of Hanna-Barbera Productions.)

*The Banana Splits*: Ronne Troup with Miguelito the monkey from the *Danger Island* segment. (Courtesy of Hanna-Barbera Productions.)

*The Bugs Bunny/Road Runner Show*:  Sylvester and Tweety. (Courtesy of Warner Communications Inc.)

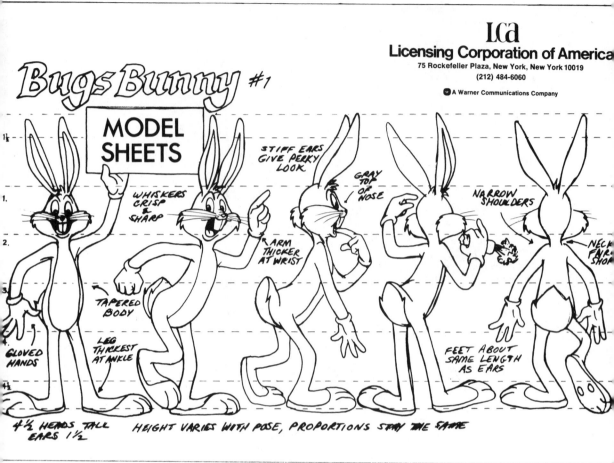

*The Bugs Bunny/Road Runner Show*: A model sheet used by animation artists. (Courtesy of Warner Communications, Inc.)

**Bunny** and **Road Runner** had been previously featured in their own individual series (1966/67).

Although Bugs Bunny and the Road Runner are stars of the series, the Warner Brothers cartoon inventory provides many additional characters, including Porky Pig, Elmer Fudd, Speedy Gonzales, Henry Hawk, Foghorn, the Leghorn, and Daffy Duck.

Bugs Bunny, known to millions the world over as a rascally rabbit, is most adept at causing trouble, and equally adept at avoiding the consequences. The Road Runner is crafty, quick and determined never to become a meal for Wile E. Coyote. No matter how many times Coyote fails to nab the Road Runner, he never gives up trying. His schemes range from incredible to impossible. He uses all manner of contraptions from the "ACME Discount Warehouse," none of which ever works—except against the hapless scavenger himself. The Road Runner uses his great speed and wits to avoid all perils awaiting him. This he does with a disarming ease that only exacerbates Coyote's fury. To add insult to injury, the Road Runner always gives a "Beep! Beep!" as he speeds by.

Over the years, parents' organizations

# Banana Bomber

The Bugs Bunny/ Road Runner Show: Sylvester and Tweetie. (Courtesy of Warner Communications, Inc.)

have often criticized this show for being too violent, particularly the *Road Runner* segment, in which Wile E. Coyote frequently sustains "great physical harm." CBS subsequently responded to this pressure by reducing the incidence of physical contact. All three networks have instructed production companies to depict less violence in children's series. Despite these changes, the show's fast-paced comedy has made it among the most popular in history. [See also: ***The Bugs Bunny Show*** (1971/72)].

## THE DUDLEY DO-RIGHT SHOW

**Sunday,** *9:30 – 10:00 a.m.: ABC*
**Debut:** *4/27/69;* **Cancellation:** *9/6/70*
**Supplier:** *Jay Ward Productions*

*Voices*
*Dudley Do-Right* . . . . . . . . . .*Bill Scott*
*Nell Fenwick* . . . . . . . . . . . . .*June Foray*
*Snidely Whiplash* . . . . . . . . . .*Hans Conried*
*Inspector Ray K. Fenwick* . .*Paul Frees*
***Other voices:*** *Bill Conrad, Walter Tetley, Skip Craig, Barbara Baldwin*
**Narrator:** *Paul Frees*

38 16mm.

*Dudley Do-Right*: Dudley Do-Right and friends. (Courtesy of P.A.T./Ward Productions.)

The setting for this animated cartoon was the early 20th century. When Dudley Do-Right, a likeable simpleton, left home to break into the movies, he lost his footing on a path and fell deep into a sewer. His upbringing dictated that he accept responsibility for what he considered a gross misdemeanor—the crime of trespass. And so he turned himself in to the Royal Canadian Mounted Police at a camp in northern Alberta. His dictum, "A Do-Right must *always* do right," was often heard on the show.

At the camp he met Inspector Fenwick, who was horrified to hear of Dudley's misdeed. In repentance the young man agreed to sign up as a Mountie. Episodes found Do-Right pursuing Snidely Whiplash, a mean and dastardly villain. Whiplash made it his business to corner and irritate Nell Fenwick, the inspector's lovely young daughter. The Mountie secretly loved young Nell, and he took great pains to rescue her. He also found many excuses to be of service to her. Sadly, Dudley yearned in vain. Sadly, Nell's love seemed reserved for his horse, Steed.

*Dudley Do-Right* began life as a segment of **Rocky and His Friends** (1959/60). He was later featured on **The Bullwinkle Show** (1961/62).

*The Go-Go Gophers:* Colonel Kit Coyote, the Sergeant, Ruffled Feather and Running Board.
(Courtesy of Leonardo-TTV Productions.)

## THE GO-GO GOPHERS

*Saturday, 8:00–8:30 a.m.: CBS*
*Debut: 9/14/68, Cancellation: 9/6/69*
*Supplier: TOTAL Television*

*Voices*
*Ruffled Feathers* . . . . . . . .*Sandy Becker*
*Running Board* . . . . . . . . .*George S. Irving*
*Colonel Kit Coyote* . . . . .*Kenny Delmar*
*The Sergeant* . . . . . . . . . .*Sandy Becker*

This cartoon was originally seen in the **Underdog** series, shown during the 1964/65 and 1966/67 seasons.

The Go-Go Gophers, Ruffled Feathers and Running Board, were two renegade Indians who lived in Gopher Gulch around 1860. Ruffled Feathers had a speech impediment, requiring his friend's interpretation. The Indians plotted the destruction of a U.S. Cavalry fort that encroached on their homeland. The bigoted Kit Coyote, colonel of the fort, constantly attempted to eliminate them.

*Wacky Races:* The Wacky contestants. (Courtesy of Hanna-Barbera Productions.)

# THE UNTAMED WORLD

*Saturday, 12:30 – 1:00 p.m.: NBC*
*Debut: 1/11/69; Cancellation: 8/30/69*
*Executive Producer: Jack Kauffman*
*Producer: Lawrence E. Neiman and Bud Wiser*
*Narrator: Philip Carey*

This mid-season documentary series, hosted by Philip Carey, used films to explore the people and animals of the remote regions of the world, including the North and South Poles.

# WACKY RACES

*Saturday, 9:30 – 10:00 a.m.: CBS*
*Debut: 9/14/68; Cancellation: 9/5/70*
*Supplier: Hanna-Barbera Productions*
*Narrator: Dave Willock*

*Voices*
Gravel Slag, Rufus
   Ruffcut, Red Max, Big
   Gruesome, Sgt. Peter
   Perfect, Rock Slag . . . .Daws Butler
Dick Dastardly, Clyde,
   Private  . . . . . . . . . . . .Paul Winchell
Luke, Blubber,
   General  . . . . . . . . . . . . John Stephenson
Rock, Muttley, Ring-A-
   Ding, Little Gruesome,
   Prof. Pat Pending  . . . .Don Messick
Penelope Pitstop . . . . . . .Janet Waldo
Others . . . . . . . . . . . . . . .Mel Blanc

Cross-country car racing was the sporty subject of this animated cartoon.

The leading characters were Dick Dastardly and his equally nasty dog, Muttley. Their car was the Mean Machine. Both characters would do anything, no matter how dirty, to win the ultimate title of "The World's Wackiest Racer." Much of the fun derived from Dastardly's nastiness to his rivals, which often backfired. Muttley displayed tremendous disloyalty by snickering boldly whenever anything went wrong for his master.

Dastardly's competitors included Pat Pending, a brilliant inventor who drove the "Convert-a-Car"; Rufus Ruffcut and Sawtooth, operators of the "Buzz Wagon"; Penelope Pitstop, "the glamour-gal of the gas pedal," who cruised in the "Compact Pussycat"; The Slag Brothers, Rock and Gravel, movers in the "Boulder Mobile"; The Aunt Hill Mob, which guided the "Bulletproof Bomb"; The Red Max, pilot of the "Crimson Haybailer"; The Gruesome Twosome, in the "Creepy Coupe"; and Luke and Blubber Bear, in their "Arkansas Chug-a-bug."

Paul Winchell, the voice of Dick Dastardly, is a famous children's entertainer and ventriloquist, and the star of many early children's TV programs. His voice has been heard in numerous cartoons.

Mel Blanc was the voice of many Warner Brothers cartoon characters, including Bugs Bunny, Porky Pig and Yosemite Sam.

Dastardly and Muttley later starred in their own series, **Dastardly and Muttley in Their Flying Machines** (1969/70).

1969-1970 Season

*The Cattanooga Cats* (left to right): Scoots, Groove and Country. (Courtesy of Hanna-Barbera Productions.)

## THE ARCHIE COMEDY HOUR

*Saturday, 11:00 – 12:00 noon:* CBS
*Debut: 9/13/69; Cancellation: 9/5/70*
*Supplier: Filmation Associates*

*Voices*
See: *The Archie Show* (*1968/69*)

The Riverdale High School students returned in this extended and reformatted show, first seen in 1968. Jughead, Reggie, Betty, Veronica and the freckle-faced hero rocked, cavorted and laughed their way through yet another series. The show introduced the character *Sabrina,* the teenage witch, and "Archie's Fun House", a feature consisting of sketches and music.

Archie and his friends returned in other formats on both CBS and NBC. These include **Archie's Fun House** (1970/71), **Archie's TV Funnies** (1971/72), *Everything's Archie* (1973/74), *The U.S. of Archie,* a program related to the bicentennial (1974), *The New Archie/Sabrina Hour* (1977/78) and *The Bang-Shang-Lalapalooza Show* (1978/79).

## THE CATTANOOGA CATS

*Saturday, 9:00 – 10:00 a.m.:* ABC
*Debut: 9/6/69; Cancellation: 9/5/70*
*Supplier: Hanna-Barbera Productions*

*Voices*
Country ................*Bill Galloway*
Groovey ................*Casey Kasem*
Scoots ..................*Jim Begg*
Kitty Jo ................*Julie Bennett*

Chessie . . . . . . . . . . . . . . . .Julie Bennett
Mildew Wolf . . . . . . . . . . . . .Paul Lynde
Lambsy . . . . . . . . . . . . . . . .Marty Ingels
Bristol Hound  . . . . . . . . . . .Allan Melvin
Phineas Fogg, Jr. . . . . . . . . .Bruce Watson
Jenny Trent . . . . . . . . . . . . .Janet Waldo
Happy . . . . . . . . . . . . . . . . .Don Messick
Smerky . . . . . . . . . . . . . . . .Don Messick
Crumdon  . . . . . . . . . . . . . . .Daws Butler
Bumbler  . . . . . . . . . . . . . . .Allan Melvin
Motor Mouse . . . . . . . . . . . .Dick Curtis
Auto Cat . . . . . . . . . . . . . . .Marty Ingels

The Cattanooga Cats was an animated cartoon featuring five singing felines, who would p-u-r-r-r notes and wink heavy lidded lashes at the audience. Thirty minutes of this hour-long show were devoted to the antics of this group on stage and on the road. The remaining half-hour was given over to three additional animated cartoons: It's A Wolf, Around the World in 79 Days and Auto Cat and Motor Mouse.

It's a Wolf followed the trials and tribulations of Lambsy, a quick-witted, curly-haired creature. He was stalked by Mildew, a tenacious wolf determined to get himself some dinner. Lambsy had a doting guardian in Bristol Hound, a self-proclaimed defender of young lambs.

Around The World in 79 Days was loosely based on the Jules Verne classic. Phineas Fogg, Jr., son of the original traveler, was determined to circumvent the globe, accompanied by his friends Jenny Trent and Happy. Opposing the trio at every turn were Crumdon and Bumbler.

Auto Cat and Motor Mouse offered a new twist to the old conflict between cat and mouse. It was essentially Tom and Jerry in a race-car setting. This cartoon later returned in a series titled **Motor Mouse** (1970/71), which also ran episodes of It's a Wolf.

Many familiar actors provided voices for these characters, including Marty Ingels, who co-starred in the prime-time comedy, I'm Dickens, He's Fester.

## DASTARDLY AND MUTTLEY IN THEIR FLYING MACHINES

**Saturday, 1:00 – 1:30 p.m.: CBS**
**Debut: 9/13/69; Cancellation: 9/3/71**
**Supplier: Hanna-Barbera Productions**

**Voices**
Dick Dastardly . . . . . . . . . . .Paul Winchell
Muttley . . . . . . . . . . . . . . . .Don Messick
Klunk . . . . . . . . . . . . . . . . . .Don Messick
The General . . . . . . . . . . . . ..Paul Winchell
Zilly . . . . . . . . . . . . . . . . . . .Don Messick

Dick Dastardly, first seen in the previous season's **Wacky Races,** appeared here as a World War One flying ace who collaborated with the enemy. His assigned task, on orders from the General, was the interception of vital communications carried by the stalwart Yankee Doodle Pigeon. He was assisted by his snickering and inept dog Muttley, and other members of the "Vulture Squadron."

## GET IT TOGETHER

**Saturday, 12:00 – 12:30 p.m.: ABC**
**Debut: 1/3/70; Cancellation: 9/6/70**
**Producer: Dick Clark Productions**
**Announcer: Sam Riddle**
**Hosts: Sam Riddle, Mama Cass Elliott**

This show presented a variety of popular musical acts. Top recording artists appeared on the program to perform their latest hit singles and other well-known songs.

The groups included Three Dog Night, Creedence Clearwater Revival, The Righteous Brothers and The Turtles. The show was co-hosted by the late Mama Cass Elliott, a vocalist with the popular band The Mamas and The Papas.

Sam Riddle is presently working on Solid Gold, a musical variety series for syndication, in conjunction with Paramount Television.

*Dastardly & Muttley* (left to right): Muttley, Dick  Dastardly, Klunk and Zilly. (Courtesy of Hanna-Barbera.)

## THE HARDY BOYS

*Saturday, 10:30 – 11:00 a.m.: ABC*
***Debut:** 9/6/69;* ***Cancellation:** 9/4/71*
***Supplier:** Filmation Associates*
***Voices:** Dallas McKennon, Jane Webb, Byron Kane*

Loosely based on the juvenile adventure novels by Franklin W. Dixon, this cartoon series updated the teenage sleuths by having them double as rock-and-roll musicians on a world tour. In each episode they solved a crime and played some popular music. A live band (called *The Hardy Boys*) performed the soundtrack for the show, playing up-beat contemporary tunes.

Dixon's highly popular duo returned in the late 1970s in a live-action, prime-time series starring Shaun Cassidy and Parker Stevenson.

## THE HECKLE AND JECKLE SHOW

*Saturday, 8:00 – 9:00 a.m.: NBC*
***Debut:** 9/6/69;* ***Cancellation:** 9/7/71*
***Supplier:** Terrytoons*
***Voices:** Paul Frees*

This cartoon series brought Terrytoons' zany twin magpies back to television.

Paul Terry created the innovative characters for *The Talking Magpies,* a 1946 theatrical cartoon. He provided them with contrasting voices— one with a Brooklyn accent, the other self-consciously British. These shorts were among the studio's most successful, and they formed the bedrock for the sale of the studio's inventory to CBS in 1955.

Heckle and Jeckle first appeared on prime time in the ***CBS Cartoon Theater*** (1956/57), hosted by Dick Van Dyke. The twins continued to appear with other Terry characters on CBS, in varying time slots from 1958 to 1960, and during the 1965/66 season. Here they played hosts to Dinky Duck, a duckling with a squeaky voice; Little Roquefort, a buck-toothed mouse with overdeveloped ears; Percy the cat; the Terry Bears (another set of twins); and Gandy Goose, a highly original character conceived in the late 1930s. The original theatrical Gandy was based on the personality of Ed Wynn, a well-known entertainer of the time. This idea was more fully developed 40 years later by Hanna-Barbera, for such series as *The Harlem Globe Trotters.*

The magpies and their companions have been featured in Claude Kirschner's syndicated series, *Terry Tell Time,* since the 1950s. Heckle and Jeckle returned to network TV in Filmation's 1979 series, *The Mighty Mouse and Heckle and Jeckle,* aired by CBS.

## HERE COMES THE GRUMP

*Saturday, 9:00–9:30 a.m.: NBC*
*Debut: 9/6/69; Cancellation: 9/4/71*
*Supplier:* DePatie-Freleng Enterprises/
   Mirisch Television

*Voices*
Princess Dawn . . .Stefanianna Christopher
Terry Dexter . . . . .Jay North
The Grump . . . . . .Rip Taylor

The setting of this animated series was a fantasy island ruled by a miserable and vindictive creature, the Grump. Plots centered on young Terry and his dog Bip, who had been magically transported to "Dawn's Kingdom."

The Grump had the power to project his misery on others. None could withstand his will power, apart from Princess Dawn. Aboard the Jolly Green Dragon, the three (Dawn, Terry and his dog) searched frantically for the crystal key that would unlock the Curse of Gloom. Each episode had the trio overcoming the inevitable obstacles put in their way by the Grump, who resolutely sought to divert them from their goal.

## HOT WHEELS

*Saturday, 10:00–10:30 a.m.: ABC*
*Debut: 9/6/69; Cancellation: 9/4/71*
*Supplier:* Pantomime Productions Corporation

*Hot Wheels*: The Hot Wheels Club. (Courtesy of Pantomime Pictures Corp.)

**Voices:** *Bob Arbogast, Melinda Casey, Susan Davis, Albert Brooks, Casey Kasem*

Jack Wheeler was the leader of the "Hot Wheel Club," a group of young racing car enthusiasts. Janet, Skip, Bud, Mickey, Tag, Art and Kip were his teenage cohorts. They put safety and common sense first, with excitement and daring next on the list.

Episodes of this animated series placed the "Hot Wheels" in competition with either "Stuff Haley and his Bombers," or "Dexter Carter and his Demons," whose objective was to "win at any price." The program emphasized good driving skills and dealt with such "non-cool" activities as smoking.

Mattel, the toy manufacturer, was a major sponsor of this show. It was no secret that they manufactured a "Hot Wheels" toy. Both the Federal Trade Commission and the Federal Communications Commission looked askance at this apparent 30-minute commercial. Although neither commission brought action, they pressured Mattel to withdraw sponsorship, resulting in the show's cancellation in 1971. Since this incident, animation studios and producers have been extremely careful to avoid connections between show subject matter and the products of sponsors.

## H.R. PUFNSTUF

*Saturday, 10:00 – 10:30 a.m.: NBC*
*Debut: 9/6/69; Cancellation: 9/4/71 (NBC)*
*Return: 9/9/72; Cancellation: 9/1/73 (ABC)*
*Supplier: Sid and Marty Krofft*

*Cast*
Jimmy . . . . . . . . . . . . . . . . . . . . .Jack Wild
Miss Witchiepoo . . . . . . . . . . . .Billie Hayes
*Others:* Joan Gerber, Felix Silla, Jerry Landon, John Linton, Angelo Rosetti, Hommy Stewart, Buddy Douglas, the Krofft Puppets.

This Saturday morning series featured live actors, with puppets in supporting roles.

Episodes centered on the adventures of Jimmy, a bright young man with a talking flute. The musical instrument (named Freddie) was made of gold. The series began with the boy and his flute taking a boat ride, far out to sea. The wicked witch, Miss Witchiepoo, cast a spell over their craft and made it disappear, forcing Jimmy to swim for his life. The boy came ashore on Living Island, where he was found by the mayor, H.R. Pufnstuf. All the while, Miss Witchiepoo was

seething, since the wreck was supposed to bring her *Freddie,* whom she wanted for her collection.

Jimmy enlisted the assistance of Judy, the frog, in his attempt to escape from the island and Witchiepoo's clutches.

Actor Jack Wild came to the series from a starring role as the Artful Dodger in *Oliver,* a movie version of Oliver Twist. H.R. Pufnstuf was the first Saturday morning children's series to be produced by Krofft Entertainment. This studio specialized in the use of puppets and became important suppliers to the schedule with such shows as **The Bugaloos** (1970/71), *Sigmund and the Sea Monsters* (1973/74) and *Land of the Lost* (1974/75). They have also ventured into prime-time with the variety shows *Donnie and Marie* (1975/76) and *Barbara Mandrell and the Mandrell Sisters* (1980/81).

## JAMBO

*Saturday, 12:00 – 12:30 p.m.: NBC*
*Debut: 9/6/69; Cancellation: 9/4/71*
*Supplier: Ivan Tors Film, Inc., in association with Thompson Enterprises and NBC-TV*
*Host: Marshall Thompson*

This live-action series investigated African wildlife. Marshall Thompson, who had been the star of *Daktari,* hosted and narrated film clips of beasts and birds in their natural habitats. Thompson's co-host was a chimpanzee named Judy.

Ivan Tors, producer of *Daktari* and the owner of Africa/USA (an amusement park), created this series. His other television credits include *Cowboy in Africa, Sea Hunt, Science Fiction Theater, Flipper,* and *Gentle Ben.* He also produced motion pictures featuring the latter two characters.

*H.R. Pufnstuff*:
H.R. Pufnstuff.
(Courtesy of
King
Features
Syndicate.)

*Jambo*: Marshall
Thompson and
pet, Judy.
(Courtesy of
Heritage
Entertainment.)

*The Pink Panther Show*: Texas Toad.

## THE PINK PANTHER SHOW

**Saturday, 9:30 – 10:00 a.m.: NBC**
**Debut:** *9/6/69;* **Cancellation:** *9/2/78 (NBC)*
**Return:** *9/9/78;* **Cancellation:** *9/1/79 (ABC)*
**Supplier:** *DePatie-Freleng Enterprises*
**Hosts:** *Lennie Schultz; The Ritts Puppets*

**Voices**
The Ant . . . . . . . . . . . . . . . . John Byner
The Aardvark . . . . . . . . . . . . John Byner
The Inspector . . . . . . . . . . . Marvin Miller
Texas Toad I . . . . . . . . . . . . Tom Holland
Texas Toad II . . . . . . . . . . . . Don Diamond
**Others:** Dave Barry, Paul Frees, Rich Little, Athena Fords
**Puppeteers:** Paul and Mary Ritts

The Pink Panther started life as an animated character in the title sequence of the Blake Edwards movie, *The Pink Panther* (1964). Edwards commissioned Fritz Freleng to provide opening and closing segments for this 1964 mystery comedy, which starred Peter Sellers.

The commission was the first for animators Freleng and David De Patie after quitting Warner Brothers in 1963. The film, distributed by United Artists, was exception-ally successful, due to Henry Mancini's music, Peter Sellers' acting and the animated sequences.

On the basis of the film's success, United Artists requested DePatie-Freleng to produce a series of animated theatrical shorts featuring the panther. These were produced at the rate of one per month, beginning with *The Pink Phink,* which surprised everyone by winning an Academy Award.

By the time NBC purchased rights to the character for Saturday morning television, a panoply of new characters had been added. One of these was The Inspector, based on Peter Sellers' Inspector Clouseau character. Subsequent characters included The Ant, the Aardvark, The Texas Toads and Misterjaws. The series has run in various time slots on both the NBC and ABC networks. In its most recent incarnation the show was hosted by the Paul and Mary Ritts puppets, a role undertaken earlier by Lennie Schultz. The show has usually run 30 minutes, but in 1976 it went to 90 minutes as *The Pink Panther Laugh-and-a-half Hour-and-a-half Show. The Pink Pink Panther Show* ran on the NBC Saturday schedule for nine seasons, and, in the fall of 1978, switched to ABC as *The All New Pink Panther Show.*

DePatie-Freleng Enterprises, once a lead-

ing supplier of Saturday morning cartoons, has produced **The Super Six** (1966/67), **Super President** (1967/68), **Here Comes the Grump** (1969/70) and **The Houndcats** (1972/73).

*The Pink Panther Show:* The star of the show and the Aardvark.

*The Pink Panther Show*: The Aardvark and Texas Toad.

(Courtesy of DePatie Freleng Enterprises, Inc.)

*Scooby-Doo, Where Are You?*: Scooby-Doo, Scrappy-Doo and Shaggy. (Courtesy of Hanna-Barbera Productions.)

## SCOOBY-DOO, WHERE ARE YOU?

**Saturday,** 10:30–11:00 a.m.: CBS
**Debut:** 9/13/69; **Cancellation:** 9/2/72
**Supplier:** Hanna-Barbera Productions

### Voices
Scooby-Doo . . . . . . . . . . . . .Don Messick
Freddy . . . . . . . . . . . . . . . .Frank Welker
Daphne . . . . . . . . . . . . . . .Heather North
Shaggy . . . . . . . . . . . . . . .Casey Kasem
Velma . . . . . . . . . . . . . . . . .Nicole Jaffe
**Others:** John Stephenson, Henry Cardin, Ann Jillian, Joan Gerber, Ted Knight, Olan Soule, Vincent Van Patten, Cindy Putnam, Pat Harrington, Frances Halop, Jim McGeorge, Mike Road

Scooby-Doo was a large, loveable, and cowardly Great Dane. He "hung out" with four California high-school students, who drove around in a car called the "Mystery Machine." The group attempted to solve

*Sky Hawks*: The Wilson Family. (Courtesy of Pantomime Pictures Corp.)

mysteries of the supernatural. At the first hint of trouble, Scooby-Doo, despite his size, would take to the hills, leaving his masters calling, "Scooby-Doo . . . Where Are You?" The mutt could always be found shivering in a closet with his head buried under his paws, or hiding behind a tree.

The Great Dane has appeared in a number of Saturday shows since 1969, including **The New Scooby-Doo Movies** (1972/73), and *Scooby's Laff-A-Lympics*, which was Saturday morning's first two-hour cartoon.

Scooby-Doo has become one of Hanna-Barbera's most widely imitated and successful creations. Merchandising tie-ins include comic books, T-shirts, costumes and other novelty items.

## SKY HAWKS

*Saturday, 11:00 – 11:30 a.m.: ABC*
*Debut: 9/6/69; Cancellation: 9/4/71*
*Supplier: Pantomime Pictures Corporation*

*Voices*
*Mike Wilson* . . . . . . . . . . . . .*Michael Rye*
*Steve* . . . . . . . . . . . . . . . . . .*Bob Arbogast*
*Caroline* . . . . . . . . . . . . . . .*Melinda Casey*
*Pappy* . . . . . . . . . . . . . . . . .*Dick Curtis*
*Baron Hughes* . . . . . . . . . .*Casey Kasem*
*Little Cindy* . . . . . . . . . . . . .*Susan Davis*

This animated series featured "Sky Hawks, Inc.," a daredevil air transport and rescue service operated by the Wilson family. Mike Wilson, a retired air force colonel and widower, was the leader of the team. He enlisted the aid of his children, Steve and Caroline, as well as his father, a World War I

*The Smokey Bear Show*: Smokey the Bear with his famous slogan. (Photo courtesy of USDA—Forest Service.)

flying ace. Pappy's foster children made up the remainder of the group.

Most of the family's clients were helicopter pilots, test pilots or charter pilots in trouble. The edge-of-the-seat plots were principally daredevil rescues. No danger could dissuade the Hawks from carrying out their stunning maneuvers.

Jack Fascinato, musical director of *Kukla, Fran and Ollie,* composed the soundtrack for this show.

## THE SMOKEY BEAR SHOW

*Saturday,* *8:30 – 9:00 a.m.: ABC*
*Debut: 9/6/69; Cancellation: 9/12/71*
*Supplier: Videocraft International/Rankin-Bass*

Created for the U.S. Forest Service by the advertising agency of Foote, Cone and Belding, Smokey the Bear is the "watchdog" of the nation's forests.

Smokey's genesis dates back to 1942, when a Park Ranger in a Western forest preserve discovered a bear cub who had been badly burned in a forest fire caused by a careless camper. He nursed the young animal (nicknamed "Smokey") back to health and subsequently presented it to the Washington Zoo. This well-publicized story brought home to many people the dangers inherent in a discarded match or cigarette, an occurrence that might bring untold terror to wild creatures and devastate forests, without the offender being the wiser.

In cooperation with the Forest Service and the War Advertising Council (the word "War" was subsequently dropped), the advertising agency conceived of an awareness campaign titled *Only You Can Prevent Forest Fires.* Its symbol was Smokey the Bear.

This animated general-interest show underscored the message begun in the ad campaign.

## WHERE'S HUDDLES?

*Wednesday, 7:30–8:00 p.m.: CBS*
*Debut: 7/1/70; Cancellation: 9/9/70*
*Supplier: Hanna-Barbera Productions*

*Voices:*
Bubba McCoy . . . . . . . . . .*Mel Blanc*
Ed Huddles . . . . . . . . . . . . .*Cliff Norton*
Marge Huddles . . . . . . . . . .*Jean VanderPyl*
Penny McCoy . . . . . . . . . . .*Marie Wilson*
Claude Pertwee . . . . . . . . .*Paul Lynde*
Fumbles . . . . . . . . . . . . . . .*Don Messick*
Mad Dog Maloney . . . . . . .*Alan Reed*
Freight Train . . . . . . . . . . . .*Herb Jeffries*
Sports announcer . . . . . . . .*Dick Enberg*

This animated prime-time summer series focussed on Ed Huddles, a fumbling pro football quarterback, and his next-door neighbor, Bubba McCoy, who played center. Both were members of a rather inept professional football team called The Rhinos.

The action on the football field was humorous and fast-moving, as the two determined athletes gave the game their all. The emphasis, however, was on their relationship, both on and off the field. There were certain similarities between this cartoon and *The Flintstones,* also created by Joseph Barbera and Bill Hanna. Both main characters were neighbors with similar interests and lifestyles.

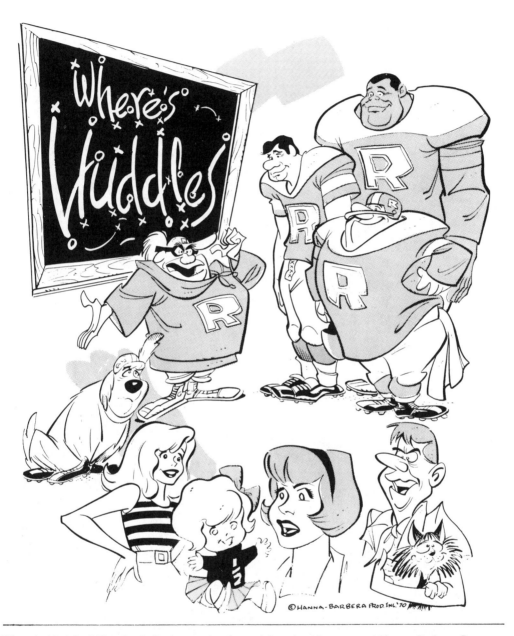

*Where's Huddles?*: The football players, family and friends. (Courtesy of Hanna-Barbera Productions.)

1970-1971 Season

# HOT DOG

**Saturday,** 12:00–12:30 p.m.: NBC
**Debut:** 9/12/70; **Cancellation:** 9/4/71
**Supplier:** Lee Mendelson/Frank Buxton Film Productions
**Narrators:** Jonathan Winters, Jo Anne Worley, Woody Allen

Although this unique series ran for only a year on Saturday mornings, it was highly respected by critics and parents. Produced in a magazine format, the show garnered a Peabody Award (1971) for excellence in children's programming.

*Hot Dog* was basically a filmed exploration of technological mysteries. These included the manufacture of such everyday items as blue jeans, bricks, footballs, and even hot dogs. Episodes explained how neon signs work, what rope is made of, and what drinking water consists of. The series frequently employed the talents of Bernie Gunther, an expert in sensory perception.

Comedians Woody Allen and Jo Anne Worley were among those who narrated segments of the show. They provided entertaining, comic twists to augment the education. Lee Mendelson, a producer of the show, was also involved in the production of the popular *Peanuts* specials. These were a series of animated cartoons based on the popular comic-strip characters.

# JOSIE AND THE PUSSYCATS

**Saturday,** 10:00–10:30 a.m.: CBS
**Debut:** 9/12/70; **Cancellation:** 8/31/74
**Supplier:** Hanna-Barbera Productions

*Voices:*
Josie . . . . . . . . . . . . . . . . .Janet Waldo
Melody . . . . . . . . . . . . . .Jackie Joseph
Valerie . . . . . . . . . . . . . . . .Barbara Pariot
Alan . . . . . . . . . . . . . . . . .Jerry Dexter
Alexander Cabot . . . . . . .Casey Kasem
Alexandra Cabot . . . . . . .Sherry Alberoni
Sebastian, the cat . . . . . .Don Messick

*Vocals:*
Josie . . . . . . . . . . . . . . . .Cathy Douglas
Valerie . . . . . . . . . . . . . . .Patricia Holloway
Cherie Moore . . . . . . . . .Cheryl Ladd

This animated cartoon series, which featured an up-temp sound track, chronicled the misadventures of an all-girl rock band.

Josie and her girls performed at concerts around the globe. Once the curtain came down, the group fraternized with the locals and involved themselves in the local comings and goings. Their musical compositions (played by a band recruited for the series) often reflected the relationships and situations in which the girls found themselves. The series title later became *Josie and the Pussycats in Outer Space,* with an obvious change in setting.

Cheryl Ladd, who provided Cherie Moore's voice, went on to ABC's *Charlie's Angels,* and a highly successful career as an actress. The Pussycats album, a collection of 16 songs taken from different episodes of the series, was released by Capitol records in 1970. The group toured during the series' run but disbanded shortly after the show was cancelled. An "extended-play" album containing four of their songs was made available as a premium by the Kellogg Corporation. Music for the series was written and arranged by Danny Janssen, Bob Ingeman and Art Mogell, under the corporate name LaLa Productions.

# LANCELOT LINK/SECRET CHIMP

**Saturday,** 9:00–10:00 a.m.: ABC
**Debut:** 9/12/70; **Cancellation:** 9/2/72
**Supplier:** Sandler-Burns-Marmer Productions

Eighteen live chimpanzees appeared in, and hosted this line-action series, which also aired cartoons. Dressed in hats and coats, the chimps were trained to emulate their

*Will the Real Jerry Lewis Please Sit Down!*: Jerry
Lewis doing it all. (Courtesy of Jerry Lewis.)

*Will the Real Jerry Lewis Please Sit Down!*: That
unmistakeable profile. (Courtesy of Jerry Lewis.)

# WOODY WOODPECKER

*Saturday, 8:30–9:00 a.m.: NBC*
*Debut: 9/12/70; Cancellation: 9/2/72*
*Supplier: Walter Lantz Productions*

*Voices: Grace Stafford Lantz (Woody Woodpecker), Paul Frees, June Foray, Walter Tetley, Daws Butler*

Walter Lantz's classic cartoon character was already 16 years old when he first appeared on television in **The Woody Woodpecker Show** (1957/1958).

Created by Ben "Bugs" Hardaway, whom Lantz had hired from Warner Brothers in the late 1930s, Woody debuted with Andy Panda in the theatrical short, *Knock, Knock* (1940). Hardaway, creator of Bugs Bunny and Daffy Duck for Warner Brothers, envisaged Woody as foil for the "goody goody" panda he had inherited from Alex Lovy. Woody's personality was so hyperactive that in one memorable movie cartoon, his neighboring animals forced the woodpecker to visit a psychiatrist. Among the many exceptional movie cartoons featuring the scraggly-combed, frenetic bird are *The Barber of Seville, Ski for Two, Who's Cookin' Who?, Pantry Panic,* and *Wet Blanket Policy.* With these and others, the Lantz studio broadened the horizons of animation. Television censorship required the trimming of the more violent scenes in the 52 movie shorts packaged for the small screen.

In this made-for-television series, Woody had evolved into a cute, non-threatening version of his former self. He was accompanied by many of his old friends: Andy Panda, Chilly Willy, Buzz Buzzard, Gabby Gator, Wally Walrus, Smedley, Knothead and Splinter. The series was hosted by Lantz himself who, in linking segments, demonstrated the technique of cartoon animation. Until he signed an exclusive contract with Warner Brothers, Mel Blanc provided Woody's voice. Since 1951, Grace Stafford, Walter Lantz's actress-wife, has provided the Woodpecker with his characteristic "Ha-ha-ha-HA-ha!" utterance.

Universal Pictures has distributed Woody's films and syndicated his cartoons throughout the world.

© 1964 WALTER LANTZ
PRODUCTIONS, INC.

*The Woody Woodpecker Show*: The indomitable
bird. (Courtesy of Walter Lantz Productions,
Inc.)

1971-1972 Season

*Archie's TV Funnies*: Dick Tracy.
(Reprinted by permission of Tribune
Company Syndicate, Inc.)

*Archie's TV Funnies*: Dick Tracy and Jo Jitsu.
(Reprinted by permission of Tribune Company
Syndicate, Inc.)

## ARCHIE'S TV FUNNIES

*Saturday,* 10:30 – 11:00 a.m.: CBS
*Debut:* 9/11/71; *Cancellation:* 9/1/73
*Supplier:* Filmation Associates

*Voices:* Jane Webb, Dallas McKennon,
Howard Morris

Archie, the freckle-faced, All-American boy,
returned with his friends from Riverdale
High for a fourth straight season on Saturday mornings. Their return was marked by
yet a new format.

*Barrier Reef*: The Great Barrier Reef off the coast of Western Australia.

✡ ✡ ✡ ✡ ✡ ✡ ✡ ✡ ✡ ✡ ✡ ✡ ✡ ✡ ✡

The show's animated characters now presented cartoon inserts. Archie and his pals were elevated to the role of host. They operated their own television station, which broadcast their favorite cartoons: *Dick Tracy, Nancy and Sluggo, Broom Hilda, The Captain and the Kids, Moon Mullins, Smokey Stover, Here Come the Drop-Outs* and *Emmy Lou*. Like Archie, these characters originated in syndicated newspaper comic strips and in comic books. Jughead, Betty, Veronica, and Reggie all took turns at introducing their favorites.

Dick Tracy had previously appeared in a series of 130 UPA-produced animated cartoons, syndicated between 1960 and 1962. The square-jawed detective had also been featured in a 1950s live-action television series.

## BARRIER REEF

*Saturday, 10:00 – 10:30 a.m.: NBC*
**Debut:** *9/11/71;* **Cancellation:** *9/2/72*
**Supplier:** *Norfolk International Productions/Ansett Transport Industries*

### Cast

| | |
|---|---|
| Capt. Chet King | Joe Jones |
| Kip King | Ken Jones |
| Joe Francis | Richard Meikle |
| Steve Goba | Howard Hopkins |
| Tracy Dean | Rowena Wallace |
| Dr. Elizabeth Hanna | Ihab Nafa |
| Diana Parker | Elli MacLure |
| Elizabeth Grant | Susanna Brett |
| Ken | Peter Adams |
| Jack | George Assang |
| Professor Barnard | Peter Carver |

This educational live-action series, one of the last non-cartoon shows to be seen on the network's Saturday schedule, was set on the Great Barrier Reef, off Western Australia. This coral wonder of the world provided an exciting backdrop for the adventures of a crew of marine biologists aboard the 220-ton windjammer, *The Endeavour*.

## THE BUGS BUNNY SHOW

*Saturday, 8:00 – 8:30 a.m.: CBS*
*Debut: 9/11/71; Cancellation: 9/1/73*
*Supplier: Warner Bros.*
*Voices: Mel Blanc*

Bugs Bunny, the inimitable, wise-cracking, cynical, know-it-all rabbit returned to the ⋯⋯ ⋯⋯ with this 30-minute show.

During the late 1940s, Jack Wrather, then head of Warner Brothers, was looking for a character to effectively compete with Walt Disney's Mickey Mouse. The task fell to Leon Schlessinger, who entered into an agreement with Wrather. In addition to Bugs Bunny, Schlessinger's cartoon studio also came up with Daffy Duck, Elmer Fudd and Porky Pig. Tex Avery, an animator for Schlessinger, is credited with the primary development of Bugs Bunny. Others, including Ben Hardaway, Charlie Thorsen, Chuck Jones, Friz Freleng, Mike Maltese and Warren Foster contributed such finishing touches as the buck teeth and the line, "Eh, What's Up, Doc?"

Bugs was featured in many theatrical cartoons before ABC brought him to prime-time television in 1960. That first Bugs Bunny Show also introduced to television other famous Warner Brothers cartoon characters: Road Runner, Wile E. Coyote, Speedy Gonzales, Sylvester, and Tweety.

All the Bugs Bunny shows to appear over the years on television have been composed of original theatrical material edited for television. Ted Pierce, Michael Maltese and Warren Foster provided the scripts.

## THE CBS CHILDREN'S FILM FESTIVAL

*Saturday, 1:00 – 2:00 p.m.: CBS*
*Debut: 9/11/71; Cancellation: 8/26/78*
*Return: February 5, 1983; Still running*
*Producer: CBS Network Production*
*Hostess: Fran Allison*
*Puppets: Burr Tillstrom*

In 1947 Burr Tillstrom established a television institution with the first appearance of **Kukla, Fran and Ollie** (1947/48). Changing perspectives at the networks during the early 1950s brought a reduction in the show's length and a vociferous response from the audience and national critics alike. At this time the Kukla, Fran and Ollie tabloid, the *Kuklapolitan Courier,* had a circulation of 200,000, and the show received thousands of letters every week. Kukla was a bald, button-nosed clown and Ollie was a highly civilized dragon. The puppets were teamed with Burr's partner, Fran Allison. The show was finally cancelled in 1957.

It was Fred Silverman, then an innovative executive at CBS, who fathered *The CBS Children's Film Festival.* He managed to woo Burr Tillstrom and his team back to television, where they provided linking passages between films, as well as commentary.

This series was devoted to both European- and Canadian-made films, many of which were made by American producers. All the films in the series contain some universal theme and appeal to children of all nationalities. Comedy and fantasy elements play a strong role in many of the films as well.

Among the films shown here (about 250 films have been shown so far) are: *Tico and the Shark, The Clown in Six Fairs, Red Baloon, Snow White, Fly Away, Dove, The Seven Ravens, Me and You, Kangaroo, The Violin,* and *The Shopping Bag Lady.* The films are dubbed in English for American audiences.

The distributors who supply the films to CBS obtain them from international film and television festivals all over the globe. Some distribution companies, including Learning Corporation of America, have also produced films themselves for the series.

The *CBS Children's Film Festival* won the Peabody Award in 1967 and the ACT Award (Action for Children's Television) for the 1971/72 season.

## CURIOSITY SHOP

**Saturday**, *11:00–12:00 noon: ABC*
**Debut**: *9/11/71;* **Cancellation**: *9/2/72*
**Return**: *9/9/72;* **Cancellation**: *9/9/73*
**Supplier**: *Sandler, Burns & Marmer Productions*
**Producer**: *Chuck Jones*

**Cast**
Gittel, the witch . . . . . . . . .Barbara Minkus
Pam . . . . . . . . . . . . . . . . . . .Pamelyn Ferdin
Gerard . . . . . . . . . . . . . . . .John Levin
Ralph . . . . . . . . . . . . . . . . .Kerry MacLane
Cindy . . . . . . . . . . . . . . . . .Jerelyn Fields
**Other voices**: *Bob Halt, Chuck Jones, Mel Blanc*

In *Curiosity Shop,* producer Chuck Jones explored the adult world by answering questions from a small group of youngsters who appeared on the show. Jones used cartoon inserts and costume drama to make his points. His characters included Gittel, the bumbling witch, and Baron Balthazar.

*Curiosity Shop,* launched on September 11, was ABC's answer to **Mr. Wizard** (1950/51), which returned to the air that same day. Ironically, Don Herbert, who played Mr. Wizard, had appeared in a 1951 WNBZ Chicago show entitled *Curiosity Shop.*

Producer Chuck Jones, vice president of children's programming for ABC, had been an award-winning animator at Warner Brothers during the 1940s. He had brought life to such characters as Bugs Bunny, the Road Runner, and Porky Pig. His theatrical cartoons include *Tom Thumb in Trouble* and *Joe Glow the Firefly.*

*Curiosity Shop*: Onamabapaeia, she just sounds the same. (Courtesy of Chuck Jones Enterprises.)

*Curiosity Shop*: Jermione, the giraffe. (Courtesy of Chuck Jones Enterprises.)

*Curiosity Shop*: The Chimp. (Courtesy of Chuck Jones Enterprises.)

*Curiosity Shop*: Halcyon. (Courtesy of Chuck Jones Enterprises.)

*Curiosity Shop* (left to right): Kerry MacLane, Jerelyn Fields and John Lenin. (Courtesy of Chuck Jones Enterprises.)

*Curiosity Shop*: Jermione, with (left to right) Kerry MacLane and John Lenin (Courtesy Of Chuck Jones Enterprises.)

*Curiosity Shop*: Balthazar. (Courtesy of Chuck Jones Enterprises.)

*Curiosity Shop* (left to right): Jerelyn Fields, John   Lenin, Kerry MacLane, and Balthazar. (Courtesy of Chuck Jones Enterprises.)

## DEPUTY DAWG

**Saturday,** *8:30 – 9:00 a.m.: NBC*
**Debut:** *9/11/71;* **Cancellation:** *9/2/72*
**Supplier:** *Terrytoons*

**Voice:** *Dayton Allen (Deputy Dawg)*

Originally syndicated in 1960, *Deputy Dawg* was created by Larz Bourne for Terrytoons. Although made for television, the cartoon brought many requests for theatrical release. Deputy Dawg was a rather simple-minded lawman in a sleepy Mississippi town. All the characters, good and bad, were animals, apart from Deputy's superior.

Terrytoon animator Ralph Bakshi directed a number of *Deputy Dawg* cartoons. He went on to receive major recognition for his innovative, full-length theatrical cartoons, including *Fritz the Cat* and *Heavy Traffic.*

## FUNKY PHANTOM

**Saturday,** *9:00 – 9:30 a.m.: ABC*
**Debut:** *9/11/71;* **Cancellation:** *9/1/73*
**Supplier:** *Hanna-Barbera Productions*

**Voices**
Jonathan Muddlemore
   (Musty) . . . . . . . . . . . . . . *Daws Butler*
April Stewart . . . . . . . . . . . . *Tina Holland*
Skip . . . . . . . . . . . . . . . . . . . *Mickey Dolenz*
Augie . . . . . . . . . . . . . . . . . . *Tommy Cook*
**Other Voices:** *Jerry Dexter, Julie Bennett*

This animated cartoon series concerned the story of Jonathan Muddlemore, a young patriot during the American Revolutionary War. Chased by Redcoats, he seeks refuge in an abandoned mansion. Unfortunately, he gets trapped inside the grandfather clock in which he has hidden.

Two centuries pass and three teenagers

caught in a storm take shelter in the house. Finding the clock, they reset it, resulting in the release of Muddlemore (Musty) as "the Spirit of '76." The young friends travel the country in this animated series to challenge injustice and discrimination and to uphold the ideals of the Declaration of Independence.

## HELP! IT'S THE HAIR BEAR BUNCH

*Saturday, 9:30–10:00 a.m.: CBS*
*Debut: 9/11/71; Cancellation: 8/31/74*
*Supplier: Hanna-Barbera Productions*

*Voices*
Hair Bear . . . . . . . . . . . . .*Daws Butler*
Bubi Bear . . . . . . . . . . . . .*Paul Winchell*

Square Bear . . . . . . . . . .*Bill Calloway*
Mr. Peevley . . . . . . . . . .*John Stephenson*
Botch . . . . . . . . . . . . . . .*Joe E. Ross*
**Other voices:** *Hall Smith, Joan Gerber, Vic Perrin, Jeannine Brown, Lennie Weinrib, Janet Waldo*

Hair, Square and Bubi were three thoroughly disgruntled grizzly bears who made their home at the Wonderland zoo. The opening of each episode signalled the bunch to vacate their cage and go off in search of fun and excitement. After half an hour of freedom, the animated trio were only too happy to scurry back to the relative safety of life in the zoo.

*Deputy Dawg:* Deputy Dawg and Bird. (Courtesy of Viacom International, Inc.)

*The Funky Phantom*: Muddlemore and Boo, his feline accomplice. (Courtesy of Hanna-Barbera Productions.)

*Help! It's the Hair Bear Bunch* (left to right): Hair Bear, Square Bear and Bubi Bear. (Courtesy of Hanna-Barbera Productions.)

*The Jackson Five*: Three of the brothers. (Courtesy of Rankin-Bass Productions.)

## THE JACKSON FIVE

**Saturday, 9:30–10:00 a.m.: ABC**
**Debut: 9/11/71; Cancellation: 9/1/73**
**Supplier:** Rankin-Bass Productions/Motown Inc.

**Voices:** The Jackson Brothers (Tito, Jackie, Michael, Marion and Jermaine)
**Other voices:** Paul Frees, Joe Cooper, Edmund Silvers

The Saturday schedule lends itself to the packaging of established sports and music stars, as witness the success of the **Harlem Globetrotters** (1970/71) and the **Osmonds** (1972/73). The popular Jackson Five singing group provided the voices for their cartoon selves. The program gave Motown records an opportunity to showcase two new songs every week.

The thin plots of the cartoons provided little more than a stage for the music.

## LIDSVILLE

**Saturday, 10:30–11:00 a.m.: ABC**
**Debut: 9/11/71; Cancellation: 9/1/73**
**Supplier:** Sid and Marty Krofft

**Cast**
Mark . . . . . . . . . . . . . .Butch Patrick
Whoo Doo . . . . . . . .Charles Nelson Reilly
Weenie the Genie . . .Billie Hayes

*Liddsville:* The Liddsville Players. (Courtesy of Krofft Entertainment.)

This was a new venture from the team that had successfully bridged the gap between marionette and live action.

Lidsville was a land inhabited by "hat people." There were helmets, Stetsons, stove pipes, caps and many more. These hats were in the employ of Whoo Doo, an evil magician. On his instructions, they detained young Mark, who had accidentally detoured to Lidsville. Mark succeeded in escaping from the magician with the help of Weenie, an amiable and sympathetic genie. Whoo Doo became enraged at the disappearance of his young captive. Each week's episode would find him plotting yet another devilish ploy to outwit Mark and put him once again under lock and key.

## MAKE A WISH

***Sunday,*** *11:30 – 12:00 noon: ABC*
***Debut:*** *9/12/71;* ***Cancellation:*** *9/5/76*
***Producer/Director:*** *Lester Cooper*
***Host:*** *Tom Chapin*

Intended for children between the ages of seven and eleven, this highly acclaimed educational series combined animation, films, songs and interviews for an absorbing blend of fantasy, history and current events. The show stressed learning and growing through the use of the imagination.

The animated cartoons were created by Al Brodax, best remembered for his work on *Yellow Submarine* and *The Beatles* television cartoon. Harry Chapin wrote the song lyrics, on average two per episode. Lester Cooper and Al Brodax were reunited for the

TV program *Animals, Animals, Animals,* hosted by Hal Linden, who played the title role in the series *Barney Miller. Make A Wish* won a Peabody Award in 1971 and an Emmy Award in 1973.

## PEBBLES AND BAMM-BAMM

*Saturday, 10:00 – 10:30 a.m.: CBS*
*Debut: 9/11/71; Cancellation: 9/2/72*
*Return: 3/8/75; Cancellation: 9/4/76*
*Supplier: Hanna-Barbera Productions*

*Voices*
Pebbles Flintstone . . . . . . . .*Sally Struthers*
Bamm-Bamm Rubble . . . .*Jay North*
Moonrock . . . . . . . . . . . . . .*Lennie Weinrib*
Fabian . . . . . . . . . . . . . . . .*Carl Esser*
Penny . . . . . . . . . . . . . . . .*Mitzi McCall*
Cindy . . . . . . . . . . . . . . . .*Gay Hartwig*
Wiggy . . . . . . . . . . . . . . . .*Gay Hartwig*

*Pebbles and Bamm-Bamm* was a spin-off of *The Flintstones,* one of the longest-running cartoon series of the 1960s. Produced by Hanna-Barbera, *The Flintstones* was an American sitcom set in a prehistoric suburb of Neanderthal America. Fred and Wilma Flintstone lived there with their baby daughter, Pebbles. Their next-door neighbors were Barney Rubble, his wife Betty, and their young son, Bamm-Bamm.

In this show, Pebbles and Bamm-Bamm are all-American prehistoric teenagers who drive back and forth on the "strip," go to Saturday night hops, the inevitable beach parties, and just hang out. Sally Struthers, Pebbles' voice, has been seen regularly in the prime-time success, *All in the Family,* and in her own show, *Gloria.* Pebbles and Bamm returned to television the following season in **The Flintstones Comedy Hour** (1972/73), which encompassed variety and music.

*Make A Wish*: Host Tom Chapin on location. (Courtesy of Lester Cooper.)

*Pebbles and Bamm-Bamm*: Fred Flintstone and his daughter Pebbles. (Courtesy of Hanna-Barbera Productions.)

## SABRINA, THE TEENAGE WITCH

**Saturday,** *11:00–11:30 a.m.: CBS*
**Debut:** *9/11/71; Cancellation: 9/1/73*
**Supplier:** *Filmation Associates*
**Voices:** *Larry Storch, Jane Webb, Dallas McKennon, John Erwin, Don Messick, Howard Morris*

Sabrina, apprentice witch, student of River-

dale High and classmate of Archie and the gang, starred here in her own show. This was a trimmed-down version of the 1970/71 series, **Sabrina and the Groovy Goolies.**

Although most anxious to use her powers to assist those in need, Sabrina wanted to keep secret her special talents, for fear of ridicule and disbelief. The situation was meant to reflect the caution and uncertainty of adolescence.

*Sabrina, the Teen-Age Witch*: Sabrina taking a ride. (Courtesy of Archie Comics Publications, Inc.)

## TAKE A GIANT STEP

**Saturday,** *10:30 – 11:30 a.m.: NBC*
**Debut:** *9/11/71;* **Cancellation:** *8/26/72*
**Supplier:** *Gloria Peropat and Giovanna Nigro*
**Hosts:** *Andrea Mays, Nancy Melendez, Nancy Wemmer, John Rucker, Bill Vliss, Linda da Silva, Heather Thomas, Chip Portocarrero, Scott Falloner, Rinky Favor, Linda Lagisola, David Kollack, Sherry Shapiro*

This live show was formatted as a discussion program with a teenage audience. With guidance and encouragement from visiting celebrities, the young hosts delved into matters of social, economic and emotional significance to teenagers.

NBC vice president George Heinemann stated that the network's intention was to "enrich a generation of children who are already information rich, but experience poor." Support was provided by Scholastic Magazines, the highly reputable publisher of educational materials. As with many critically acclaimed, "educational" programs, *Take A Giant Step* lasted only a year.

*Take a Giant Step:* Three young hosts of the show. (Courtesy of Giovanna Nigro.)

# 1972-1973 Season

*The Amazing Chan and the Chan Clan*: The Chan Clan. (Courtesy of Hanna-Barbera.)

## THE AMAZING CHAN AND THE CHAN CLAN

**Saturday,** *9:00 – 9:30 a.m.: CBS*
**Debut:** *9/9/72;* **Cancellation:** *9/1/74*
**Supplier:** *Hanna-Barbera Productions*

**Voices**
Charlie Chan . . . . . . . . .*Keye Luke*
Stanley Chan  . . . . . . . .*Stephen Wong,*
                            *Lennie Weinrib*
Henry Chan  . . . . . . . . .*Bob Ito*
Suzie Chan  . . . . . . . . . .*Virginia Ann Lee,*
                            *Cherylene Lee*
Alan Chan . . . . . . . . . . .*Brian Tochi*
Anne Chan  . . . . . . . . . .*Leslie Kumamota,*
                            *Jodie Foster*
Tom Chan . . . . . . . . . . .*Michael Takamoto,*
                            *John Gunn*
Flip Chan . . . . . . . . . . . .*Jay Jay Jue,*
                            *Gene Andrusco*

Nancy Chan  . . . . . . . .*Debbie Jue,*
                            *Beverly Kushida*
Mimi Chan  . . . . . . . . .*Leslie Kawai,*
                            *Cherylene Lee*
Scooter Chan  . . . . . . . .*Robin Toma,*
                            *Michael Morgan*
Chu Chu, the dog  . . . .*Don Messick*
**Other voices:** *Lisa Gerritsen, Hazel Sher-mit, Janet Waldo, Len Wood*

Charlie Chan was the inscrutable detective-hero of a series of novels and movies during the 1930s. Charlie had ten divinely provided children (in this animated remake of the movie features four of them were girls). He solved seemingly unsolvable puzzles, usually despite the children's assistance.

# AROUND THE WORLD IN 80 DAYS

*Saturday, 12:00 – 12:30 p.m.: NBC*
*Debut: 9/9/72; Cancellation: 9/1/73*
*Supplier: Hanna-Barbera Productions*

**Voices**
Phileas Fogg . . . . . . . . . . . .Alistair Duncan
Belinda . . . . . . . . . . . . . . . .Janet Wald
Jean Passepartout . . . . . . . .Ross Higgins
Mister Fix . . . . . . . . . . . . . .Max Obistein
*Other voices: Owen Weingott*

Based on the Jules Verne classic and its
movie adaptation, this Australian animated
cartoon depicted the joys of balloon travel.

The show's two main characters were
Phileas Fogg and Belinda, who wanted to be
married. They were prevented from doing
so by Lord Maze, Belinda's disapproving
uncle. To prove his worthiness to his pomp-
ous relative, Phileas challenged him to a
wager that he could travel the circumference
of the earth in 80 days. Maze scoffed at the
venture. Maze hired Mister Fix, an evil ne'er-
do-well, to sabotage Phileas' journey. But
Fogg and his assistant Passepartout never-
theless traveled around the world by balloon, beating the clock. And, of course,
Fogg won Belinda's hand.

# THE BARKLEYS

*Saturday, 10:30 – 11:00 a.m.: NBC*
*Debut: 9/9/72; Cancellation: 9/1/73*
*Supplier: DePatie-Freleng Enterprises*

**Voices**
Arnie Barkley . . . . . . . . . . .Henry Corden
Agnes Barkley . . . . . . . . . .Joan Gerber
Terri Barkley . . . . . . . . . . . .Julie McWhirter
Chester Barkley . . . . . . . . .Steve Lewis
Roger Barkley . . . . . . . . . . .Gene Andrusco

Archie and Edith Bunker, mainstays of the
highly successful prime-time situation comedy *All in the Family*, were the models for

this Saturday morning animated cartoon. In
the early 1970s the networks looked to
prime-time for models that could be adapted
for juveniles.

*The Barkleys* were a family of middle-
class dogs! Arnie, the opinionated father,
drove a bus. He rarely attempted to com-
prehend anything beyond his bigoted vision.
His children, modeled after typical late-1960s
flower children, had little patience for the
intransigence of their elders.

# THE BRADY KIDS

*Saturday, 10:30 – 11:00 a.m.: ABC*
*Debut: 9/16/72; Cancellation: 8/31/74*
*Supplier: Filmation Associates*

**Voices**
Marcia Brady . . . . . . .Maureen McCormick
Greg Brady . . . . . . . .Barry Williams
Janice Brady . . . . . . .Eve Plumb
Peter Brady . . . . . . . .Christopher Knight
Cindy Brady . . . . . . . .Susan Olsen
Bobby Brady . . . . . . .Michael Lookinland
*Others: Larry Storch, Jane Webb*

This animated cartoon was based on the
popular prime-time series, *The Brady
Bunch*. The show focused on the children,
who had moved to a tree house from their
suburban dwelling. An extroverted and self-
reliant sibling group, they had a great sense
of adventure. The vocals were provided by
the original cast of the prime-time series.

# FAT ALBERT AND THE COSBY KIDS

*Saturday, 12:30 – 1:00 p.m.: CBS*
*Debut: 9/9/72; Still Running*
*Supplier: Filmation Associates*

*Voices: Bill Cosby, Gerald Edwards, Keith
Allen, Pepe Brown, Jon Crawford, Lane
Vaux, Erika Carroll*

*The Brady Kids* (left to right): Greg, Marcia, Peter, Janice, Bobby and Cindy. (Courtesy of Paramount Pictures Corp.)

Actor/comedian Bill Cosby, who has a basketball player's height and a seven-year-old's impish grin, was the inspiration for this highly successful cartoon show. Lou Scheimer and Norman Prescott of Filmation approached Cosby with the idea of a series featuring a group of disenfranchised kids. The show would depict their subsequent establishment of self-esteem and educational proficiency.

Fat Albert is a large and likeable lad who is looked up to by his buddies, Rudy, Weird Harold, Edward, Mush Mouth, Donald, Becky and Russell. The Fat Albert gang helps other teenagers (and occasionally adults) to identify problems and solve them before they become insurmountable.

The show's producers engaged a number of educators from UCLA to work directly with the studio's writers on story detail and character development. This dedication and unity of purpose paid off. The series has received critical acclaim from parents and educators alike. The show's ratings have been consistently strong, and it is still running more than 10 years after its debut.

Unlike other successful shows, this one has not spawned an abundance of merchandise. Cosby's producers have guarded the show's integrity by granting only a few licenses for products, based on actual shows, and then only for educational purposes. Cosby has been seen in many film and television productions, as well as commercials. In the late 1970s, he was named "Ad Spokesman of the Year." His sincerity and gentle sense of humor have made him a remarkably popular figure.

## THE FLINTSTONES COMEDY HOUR

*Saturday, 11:00–12:00 noon: CBS*
*Debut: 9/9/72; Cancellation: 1/19/74*
*Supplier: Hanna-Barbera Productions*

## Voices

Fred Flintstone . . . . . . . . Alan Reed
Barney Rubble . . . . . . . . Mel Blanc
Wilma Flintstone . . . . . . Jean VanderPyl
Betty Rubble . . . . . . . . . Gary Hartwig
Pebbles Flintstone . . . . . Mickey Stevens
Bamm Bamm Rubble . . . Jay North
Moonrock . . . . . . . . . . . . Lennie Weinrib
Penny . . . . . . . . . . . . . . . Mitzi McCall
Fabian . . . . . . . . . . . . . . Carl Esser
Schleprock . . . . . . . . . . . Don Messick
Wiggy . . . . . . . . . . . . . . . Gary Hartwig
Bronto . . . . . . . . . . . . . . Lennie Weinrib
Zonk . . . . . . . . . . . . . . . . Mel Blanc
Noodles . . . . . . . . . . . . . John Stephenson
Stub . . . . . . . . . . . . . . . . Mel Blanc

The success of the original *Flintstones* series and its spin-off, **Pebbles and Bamm Bamm** (1971/72), brought the entire family back to the Saturday schedule in this expanded one-hour show. Added were a bevy of background characters.

Initially derived from *The Honeymooners*—Jackie Gleason's legendary prime-time situation comedy, this animated cartoon was set in the suburb of Bedrock in prehistoric America. The additional cast members were mostly friends of the teenage Pebbles and Bamm Bamm. The expanded format included a new musical group, The Bedrock Rockers.

In 1973 the title of the series was changed to *The Flintstones Show,* although the format remained the same.

*Fat Albert and the Cosby Kids*: Fat Albert and the gang. (Courtesy of Filmation Associates.)

*Josie and the Pussycats in Outer Space*: The gang being followed. (Courtesy of Hanna-Barbera Productions.)

## THE HOUNDCATS

**Saturday, 9:30–10:00 a.m.: NBC**
**Debut: 9/9/72; Cancellation: 9/1/73**
**Supplier: DePatie-Freleng Enterprises**

### Voices
Studs . . . . . . . . . . . . . . . . . . .Daws Butler
Muscle Mutt . . . . . . . . . . . . . .Aldo Ray
Rhubarb . . . . . . . . . . . . . . . .Arte Johnson
Puddy Puss . . . . . . . . . . . . . .Joe Besser
Ding Dong . . . . . . . . . . . . . .Stu Gilliam

According to the old saw, cats and dogs just don't mix. This show proved that traditional enemies could bury the hatchet and pool their resources to fight evil. The format was a parody of secret-agent TV shows and movies. The Houndcats' adventures inevitably resulted in slapstick chaos.

## JOSIE AND THE PUSSYCATS IN OUTER SPACE

**Saturday, 10:30–11:00 a.m.: CBS**
**Debut: 9/9/72; Cancellation: 1/20/74**
**Supplier: Hanna-Barbera Productions**

### Voices
Josie . . . . . . . . . . . . . . . .Janet Waldo
Melody . . . . . . . . . . . . . .Jackie Joseph
Valerie . . . . . . . . . . . . . . .Barbara Pariot
Alan . . . . . . . . . . . . . . . . .Jerry Dexter
Alexandra Cabot . . . . . . .Sherry Alberoni
Alexander Cabot . . . . . . .Casey Kasem
Sebastian . . . . . . . . . . . .Don Messick
Bleep . . . . . . . . . . . . . . . .Don Messick

### Vocals
Josie . . . . . . . . . . . . . . . .Cathy Douglas
Valerie . . . . . . . . . . . . . .Patricia Holloway
Cherie Moore . . . . . . . . .Cheryl Ladd

This cartoon was simply a reworking of **Josie and The Pussycats** (1971/72).

The rock group was posing in front of a spacecraft for publicity photographs, when Alexandra accidentally fell against a "blast-off" mechanism. The result was a trip to the farthest galaxies. On Earth they had divided their time equally between singing and solving crimes, which is what they did in outer space, skipping from planet to planet.

## KID POWER

*Saturday, 11:30–12:00 noon: ABC*
*Debut: 9/16/72; Cancellation: 9/1/74*
*Supplier: Rankin/Bass Productions*

*Voices: John Gardiner, Jay Silverheels, Jr., Allan Melvin. Michele Johnson, Charles* Kennedy, Jr., Carey Wong, Jeff Thomas, Gregg Thomas, Gary Shapiro

Based on the widely syndicated comic strip *Wee Pals,* created by Morrie Turner, this cartoon series focused on the Rainbow Club. A world-wide organization, the club had a membership of adolescents of all cultural and ethnic backgrounds.

Episodes showed the kids doing their utmost to improve their immediate environment. The objective was to demonstrate that all children, regardless of background, could work together successfully. The program encouraged team work, responsibility and sharing. Prejudice and moral values were also explored.

The program was similar to **Fat Albert and the Cosby Kids** (1972/73), but it lacked the neighborhood identity or the charisma of Bill Cosby.

*Kid Power:* The Rainbow Club. (Courtesy of Rankin-Bass Productions.)

*The New Scooby-Doo Movies*: Jonathan Winters and Scooby-Doo. (Courtesy of Hanna-Barbera Productions.)

## THE NEW SCOOBY-DOO MOVIES

**Saturday,** *9:30 – 10:30 a.m.: CBS*
**Debut:** *9/9/72; Cancellation: 8/31/74*
**Supplier:** *Hanna-Barbera Productions*

**Voices:** *Don Messick, Frank Welker, Heather North, Casey Kasem, Nicole Jaffe*

Scooby-Doo, a loveable Great Dane who ran from his own shadow, was the permanent companion to a group of inquisitive high-school students. This was the loveable Dane's second series—the first was **Scooby-Doo Where Are You?** (1969/70), where Scooby had developed his reputation for canine cowardice. This expanded show included such cartoon characters as *Batman and Robin*, the *Three Stooges,* and **The Harlem Globetrotters** (1970/71 season).

*The Osmonds:* The Osmond Brothers. (Courtesy of Comworld Productions.)

## THE OSMONDS

*Saturday, 9:00 – 9:30 a.m.: ABC*
*Debut: 9/9/72; Cancellation: 9/1/74*
*Supplier: Rankin-Bass Productions*
*Voices: Allen, Jay, Jimmy, Donny, Merril*
  *and Wayne Osmond; Paul Frees*

The Osmond Brothers arrived hard on the heels of **The Jackson Five,** who had come to ABC's Saturday morning line-up during the 1971/72 season. In this cartoon series, the popular rock siblings (without sister Marie) functioned as goodwill ambassadors, appointed by the United States Music Committee. They traveled extensively and performed in different countries, to promote understanding and international harmony. Their task was somewhat complicated, however, as they often found themselves involved in foreign intrigues.

A potential hit song was sung in each episode, providing a trailer for an upcoming release.

## ROMAN HOLIDAYS

*Saturday, 10:00 – 10:30 a.m.: NBC*
*Debut: 9/9/72; Cancellation: 9/1/73*
*Supplier: Hanna-Barbera Productions*

*Voices*
Gus Holiday . . . . . . . . .*Dave Willock*
Laurie Holiday . . . . . . . .*Shirley Mitchell*
Precocia . . . . . . . . . . . . .*Pamelyn Ferdin*
Happius . . . . . . . . . . . . . .*Stanley Livingston*
Mr. Evictus . . . . . . . . . . .*Dom DeLuise*
Mr. Tycoonius . . . . . . . .*Hal Smith*
Brutus, the lion . . . . . . .*Daws Butler*
Groovia . . . . . . . . . . . . . .*Judy Strangis*
Herman . . . . . . . . . . . . . .*Hal Peary*
Henrietta . . . . . . . . . . . . .*Janet Waldo*

There is a certain resemblance between this animated cartoon series and the highly successful **The Flintstones** (1960/61), both produced by Hanna-Barbera. The Holiday family were citizens of Rome in 63 A.D. As with the prehistoric Fred and Wilma

*Roman Holidays*: Brutus the lion and the Holiday family. (Courtesy of Hanna-Barbera Productions.)

*Runaround*: Paul Winchell and young contestants. (Courtesy of Paul Winchell.)

Flintstone, they were faced with all the usual problems of a growing family, including taxes, transportation and education.

# RUNAROUND

*Saturday, 11:30–12:00 noon: NBC*
*Debut: 9/9/72; Cancellation: 9/4/76*
*Supplier: Heatter-Quigley Productions*
*Host: Paul Winchell*
*Announcer: Kenny Williams*

Ventriloquist Paul Winchell had been a force in children's television since the 1940s. He and his carved companions Jerry Mahoney and Knucklehead Smith hosted this children's quiz game show.

Nine young contestants participated in each game. The competition was gradually reduced to two players. Contestants were eliminated when they failed to answer questions correctly. Prizes were awarded to the winner.

# SATURDAY SUPERSTAR MOVIE

*Saturday, 9:30–10:30 a.m.: ABC*
*Debut: 9/9/72; Cancellation: 8/25/73*
*Supplier: Hanna-Barbera Productions*

This ABC experiment with a new format for Saturday mornings aired original animated films. The subject matter was taken from comic books, television series, motion pictures, literature and real life. Programs included *Lassie, Nanny and the Professor, Gidget Makes the Wrong Connection, Popeye, Oliver Twist* and *Say Hey, Kid,* the last an animated biography of Willie Mays, using the baseball player's actual voice for the soundtrack.

## SEALAB 2020

*Saturday, 11:00–11:30 a.m.: NBC*
*Debut: 9/9/72; Cancellation: 9/1/73*
*Supplier: Hanna-Barbera Productions*

*Voices*
Capt. Mike Murphy . . . . .John Stephenson
Dr. Paul Williams . . . . . . .Ross Martin
Hal . . . . . . . . . . . . . . . .Jerry Dexter
Gail . . . . . . . . . . . . . . . .Ann Jillian
Ed . . . . . . . . . . . . . . . . .Ron Pinchard
Bobby Murphy . . . . . . . .Josh Albee
Salli Murphy . . . . . . . . . .Pamelyn Ferdin
Sparks . . . . . . . . . . . . . .Bill Callaway
Jamie . . . . . . . . . . . . . . .Gary Shapiro
Mrs. Thomas . . . . . . . . .Olga James

Ecology was emphasized in this animated adventure series, which focused on 21st-century Oceanauts.

Sealab 2020 was a scientific experimental complex constructed on the ocean floor. 250 people participated in the maintenance of the giant laboratory and its diverse operations. There was some resemblance to Jules Verne's concept of the Nautilus in his novel, *20,000 Leagues under the Sea.* There were also elements of the Atlantis "lost-continent" theory.

Ross Martin had previously co-starred in the popular TV series *The Wild, Wild West.*

## TALKING WITH A GIANT

*Saturday, 12:30–1:00 p.m.: NBC*
*Debut: 9/9/72; Cancellation: 9/1/73*
*Producer/Director: Gloria Peropat*
*Hosts: Andrea Mays, Nancy Melendez, Nancy Wemmer, John Rucker, Bill Bliss, Linda Lloyd da Silva, Heather Thomas, Chip Portocarrero, Scott Falloner, Rinky Favor, Linda Lagisola, David Kollack, Sherry Shapiro*

This live series was the successor to ***Take a Giant Step*** (1971/72), a short-lived talk show out of the mold of ***Curiosity Shop*** (1971/72) and ***Mr. Wizard*** (1950/51).

NBC vice president George Heinemann conceived the program as helping "children make their own value judgments and build oral skills." Leading lights from many fields appeared and answered questions from a small group of articulate teenagers. Subjects such as philosophy, religion, emotions and sexual roles were discussed. The youngsters also hosted their own show, which was produced by Scholastic Magazines.

*Sealab 2020*: Imminent danger awaits two divers.   (Courtesy Hanna-Barbera.)

# Index